Quest *for the* Cup

The Detroit Red Wings' Unforgettable Journey to the 1997 Stanley Cup

By Cynthia Lambert, Bob Wojnowski, Joe Falls, Jerry Green
and The Detroit News Sports Staff

Edited by Mike Bynum

The Detroit News

GANNETT

The Detroit News

MARK SILVERMAN, *Publisher and Editor*

CHRISTINA BRADFORD, *Managing Editor*

FRANK LOVINSKI, *Deputy Managing Editor*

PHIL LACIURA, *Executive Sports Editor*

CHRISTOPHER KOZLOWSKI, *Assistant Managing Editor Design/Graphics*

DAVID KORDALSKI, *Design/Graphics Editor*

STEVEN FECHT, *Director of Photography*

Acknowledgements

RESEARCH ASSISTANCE
Alan Whitt, Rob Allstetter, Mike Katz, Chris Farina, Karen Van Antwerp and Terry Jacoby

Chapters 4, 5, 6 and 7 reprinted by permission of The Detroit News. Copyright© 1997 by The Detroit News. All rights reserved.

ISBN 1-57243-258-6

COVER DESIGN
Christopher Kozlowski

BOOK DESIGN
Christopher Kozlowski, David Kordalski, Dan Janke, Richard Epps and Darryl Swint

PHOTO EDITING
Michael Brown, Jan Lovell

Published for The Detroit News by:
Triumph Books
644 South Clark Steet
Chicago, Illinois 60605
(312) 939-3330

For more information about other sports publications in the Triumph Books library, please call 1-800-335-5523.

Contents

INTRODUCTION *by Phil Laciura, The Detroit News Executive Sports Editor*

STANLEY CUP FINALS PHOTO GALLERY 4

JOURNEY TO GREATNESS 10

1996-97: TEAM OF DESTINY 18

TIMES HAVE CHANGED SINCE THE CUP'S LAST VISIT 26

THE STANLEY CUP FINALS 36

    GAME 1, *Wings vs. Flyers, May 31, 1997* 38

    GAME 2, *Wings vs. Flyers, June 3, 1997*..........................46

    GAME 3, *Wings vs. Flyers, June 5, 1997* 54

    GAME 4, *Wings vs. Flyers, June 7, 1997* 64

STEVE YZERMAN: THE CAPTAIN 78

SCOTTY BOWMAN: THE COACH 86

RED WINGS PHOTO ROSTER....................................94

Heaven *in* Hockeytown

Darren McCarty

Brendan Shanahan

Steve Yzerman

Slava Fetisov gives goaltender Mike Vernon a congratulatory hug.

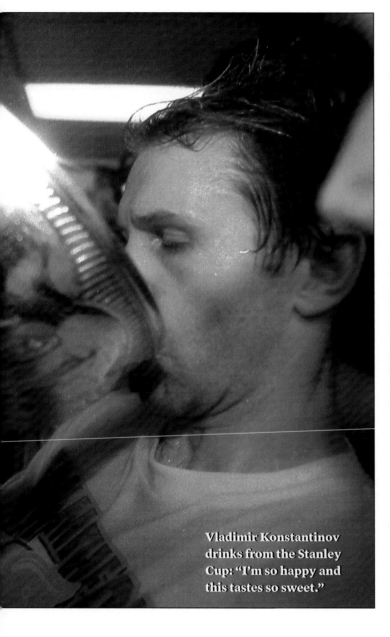

Vladimir Konstantinov
drinks from the Stanley
Cup: "I'm so happy and
this tastes so sweet."

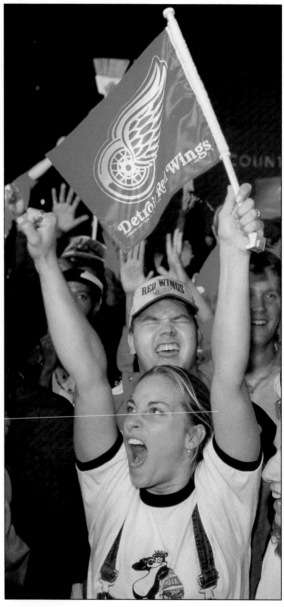

Savoring
the Cup

"I KNOW IN MY HEART MY DAD IS UP THERE HELPING HIS BELOVED Wings bring home the Stanley Cup! He never gave up on them."

That e-mail message from Connie Littman of Shelby Township, Mich., demonstrates why this state has gone slightly bonkers over the Wings' Stanley Cup victory.

Hockey fans always have been known for their loyalty. And few have suffered more from generation to generation than those in Michigan.

It wasn't only because the team had not won the Cup since 1955. It was the way it lost. It was the 16 out of 17 losing seasons from 1970-71 through 1985-86. It was the lack of hope.

That changed dramatically in 1986 when owner Mike Ilitch, who desired a Cup as much as his long-suffering fans, hired Jacques Demers as coach. Demers quickly named Steve Yzerman the youngest captain in franchise history.

The team was suddenly competitive, but the frustration continued.

After two exhilarating trips to the conference finals, Demers was fired after missing the playoffs.

Bryan Murray took over, but the Wings faltered in the playoffs in the same manner his teams in Washington did.

Murray became general manager in 1994, and Scotty Bowman, winner of six Stanley Cups, was hired as coach to end the frustration. It only grew. Bowman and Murray bickered, the Wings failed to land a top goalie for the playoffs and were shockingly ousted by San Jose.

Murray was fired. Bowman traded for Mike Vernon and led the team to the Cup Finals in 1995. But New Jersey won in a sweep. The next year, the Wings won an NHL-record 62 regular-season games, but were no match for Colorado in the Western Conference finals.

Everything about the 1996-97 season was magical. The Wings made a big trade, landing Brendan Shanahan from Hartford. Darren McCarty beat up the Wings' nemesis, Claude Lemieux of Colorado. The Wings humbled the Avalanche in the

Western Conference finals and swept the Flyers behind Yzerman and Vernon. Bowman was a genius again.

Throughout the roller-coaster ride of the franchise, The News has been there.

We, too, have history. Joe Falls has been a sports writer for 50 years. Jerry Green has as many memories from Olympia as he does from Joe Louis Arena.

Their writing helped give perspective to the rest of our coverage.

It was a team effort. Cynthia Lambert, the Wings' beat reporter since 1986, worked tirelessly. Nicknamed "The Shadow" by the Wings because she is always around the team, she had fewer off days during the season than many Wings players. And, like Vernon, she also had support.

Columnist Bob Wojnowski wrote extensively about the Wings and was credited with convincing the team to sign free-agent Joe Kocur, who had been playing in a local beer league.

Columnist Terry Foster, an NBA and NFL expert, proved his versatility. John Niyo wrote outstanding features and stories all season as Lambert's backup. John U. Bacon pro-

vided in-depth features. The rest of the coverage included great work from Dave Dye, Dave Goricki, Ted Kulfan, Vartan Kupelian and others.

The photo department, under the direction of Steve Fecht, produced quality work on a daily basis.

The design and graphics department, under the leadership of Chris Kozlowski and David Kordalski, showed why it is annually recognized as one of the nation's best.

And then there is our version of The Grind Line. Our copy desk and inside managers who on many game nights started work at 4 p.m. and didn't leave the building until 6 a.m. They are: Rob Allstetter, Jeff Barr, Art Brooks, Bev Eckman, Rick Epps, Brian Handley, Terry Jacoby, Dan Janke, Darryl Swint, Robert Jones, Michael Katz, Matt Rennie, Duke Ritenhouse, Jim Russ, Jeff Samoray, David Srinivasan, Jim Thompson, Alan Whitt, Steve Wilson and Craig Yuhas.

This book, much like the success of the Wings, was a team effort.

I hope you enjoy it.

Phil Laciura
Executive sports editor
The Detroit News

Journey to Greatness

The Red Wings' quest for the Cup

By Bob Wojnowski

The Detroit News

In a dark, dingy dressing room in the New Jersey swamplands, it took root. It was planted in the hearts and psyches of dejected players, some with eyes red, some with heads down, all suffering from abject humiliation. Out on the ice, the New Jersey Devils celebrated, and as player after player hoisted the Stanley Cup, the cheers thundered.

Through thick concrete walls, the Red Wings could hear the noise, muffled but so clear, close but so distant. Every now and then, someone, a player, a fan, would run past the open door and let out a whoop that would echo around the room, where players sat, staring at the floor.

Down a hallway, Steve Yzerman, dressed in gray, leaned heavily against a wall. It was an all-too familiar pose, and he offered an all-too familiar response.

"It's just hard to watch someone celebrate at your expense," he said. "You know what I was thinking all during the third period, when all that excitement was building? I kept wishing I was in their shoes."

For 42 years, it was that way, another season gone, another summer spent coveting the other guy's footwear, and hardware. It was late June 1995, and the Wings, heavily favored, were swept in the Stanley Cup Finals by New Jersey. After a 5-2 loss in Game 3, Scotty Bowman had

---

The Red Wings suffered two years of abuse after losing to New Jersey in the 1995 Stanley Cup Finals.

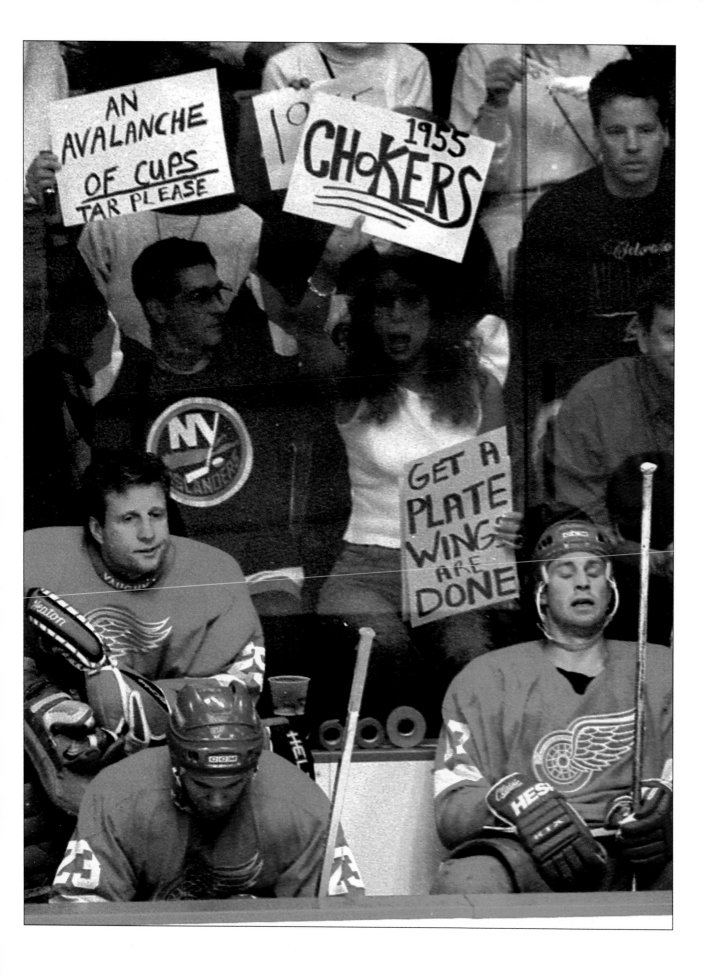

called it "an embarrassment to the National Hockey League."

Game 4 was not much better, another 5-2 loss. Mike Vernon had allowed soft goals as his defense crumbled around him. The Wings, unfamiliar with the Devils' trapping defense, had panicked, had abandoned all team concepts. Bowman failed to inspire them and no player stepped up and led.

In the dressing room, Darren McCarty was in tears. Kris Draper stared straight ahead.

"To walk down the line and shake (the Devils') hands, you see the tears of joy in their eyes, and you realize how precious it is to win the Cup," Draper said. "We have to look at it as a learning experience. You feel for the older guys who might never have this opportunity again."

A hunger must start somewhere, usually in the most profound emptiness. And really, this is where it began, sown in the ultimate failure. To understand how the 1996-97 Red Wings became Stanley Cup champions, to know why Yzerman finally took that long-awaited skate, you must know what drove them, what taught them, who led them.

Three people stand out — the captain, the coach, the goalie.

Bowman was the one with the blueprint, with six Stanley Cup rings. In his first season in Detroit, the top-seeded Wings were shocked in the first round by San Jose. In a sense, Bowman had given them the rope and let them use it as they wished. When the Wings abandoned the defensive plan, the Sharks completed the upset, and Bowman had their attention.

He demanded defense and commanded respect, and beginning with the Jersey failure, he seized power

Vladimir Konstantinov's rugged defensive play would be one of the keys in the Red Wings' return to the Stanley Cup Finals.

and stamped his imprint on the team. He was dictatorial, and at times, players and management resisted. But Bowman was driven by history, by the chance to become the first coach to win Cups with three different franchises, to take his place in NHL lore and deliver on Mike Ilitch's mandate.

Vernon, the goalie, was driven by something more personal. He had been booed out of Calgary, even after leading the Flames to the 1989 Cup. He came to Detroit with a bit of a chip, and when he shouldered much

of the blame for the Jersey debacle, his resolve grew.

Yzerman was the one who adjusted the most, and after an uneasy 1995 summer, he arrived at the start of the following season unsure of his future. Bowman had decided not to make significant changes, but now as the season dawned, rumors swirled that he was shopping Yzerman around the league. Ottawa, Yzerman's hometown, was interested.

This was Bowman's dangerous time, and a critical juncture for the franchise. Operating with deliberate calculation, he contemplated whether to trade Yzerman, whether the move was necessary to alter the makeup of the team, whether the Wings could win with Yzerman as their leader. He contemplated it all ... until Opening Night 1995.

That's when the fans spoke, and everyone listened. When announcer Bud Lynch introduced Yzerman before the game, the applause shook the building ... the fans stood ... Yzerman nodded uncomfortably ... and in a bit of comic relief, Bowman waved to the crowd and ducked from the bench down a tunnel, as if to say, "I'll leave if you don't like me."

It wasn't necessary for Bowman to leave, only for him to understand. The mandate was this: Win a Cup, but do it with the captain. Trade rumors died, and from that point, Bowman and Yzerman seemed more willing to work together, to understand each other. If the Wings were to win a title, they needed the coach, the captain and the goalie, and as they headed into the 1995-96 season, they still had so much to learn.

Championship teams generally take three steps. The first is Foundation-Building, and the Wings constructed theirs in the early 1990's. The second is Learning at the Highest Level, and the Wings were now deep into the process, headed toward the third step — Final Refining.

History is a wonderful teacher. So is failure. The Wings knew their history, were reminded of the franchise's 1955 collar constantly, and they had known failure. They had been regular-season wizards that lacked stamina, strength or the will to win it all, so in an astounding effort, they set out to prove everybody wrong.

Trouble was, they set out too quickly, as if trying to win the Stanley Cup in January. Their 62 victories were an NHL record, a picture of joyless resolve. Nothing could satiate them, nothing could stop them, nothing but their own obsession.

This was Bowman's biggest mistake. He constructed such an efficient team, it had no idea how to react when adversity struck in the playoffs. The Wings lulled themselves into false security, and spent far too much energy chasing the regular-season record.

By the trading deadline, the Wings were so dominant, Bowman couldn't bring himself to pull the trigger to make them bigger and stronger, an old mantra that had been buried under the tide of success. The only significant moves were to acquire Igor Larionov for Ray Sheppard, and Kirk Maltby for youngster Dan McGillis. Both deals would pay dividends during the regular season but not in the playoffs, not yet.

And for everything they accomplished, the Wings entered the playoffs without a clear-cut No. 1 goalie. Osgood started 50 games, Vernon 32. Both played well, and they shared the Jennings Trophy for fewest goals allowed. But it was difficult to tell if they were that good, or Detroit's defense was that disciplined. Like most of the Wings, neither goalie had faced a major test, and now the playoffs beckoned.

As the Wings prepared to meet Winnipeg in the first round of the 1995-96 season, they were wearing that familiar burden of heavy favorites, and didn't seem to mind.

"It's just the way sports is, why get all tense about it?" Darren McCarty said. "It'd be tough to accept if we felt we're overachievers. We know we have to win it. If we didn't think we could, that'd be pressure. Maybe we're putting a lot of pressure on ourselves, but we are having fun."

He said it almost like he had to convince himself. Yes, winning was fun for the Wings. But Bowman drove them ruthlessly, and when Winnipeg goalie Nikolai Khabibulin began to make huge saves, the Wings were like spelling bee whizzes suddenly drawing tougher words than they anticipated.

The Jets extended the Wings to six games, and after a clumsy goalie rotation, Bowman settled on Osgood. Then came St. Louis, and trouble — Lesson No. 2 in overconfidence. After the Wings won the first two games and made superstars Wayne Gretzky and Brett Hull look gray and frayed, they couldn't finish as quickly as they needed to.

Game 3 in St. Louis went to overtime, where Keith Primeau misfired on a breakaway moments before the Blues scored the winner. Instead of a possible sweep, the Wings were extended, and energy was drained. St. Louis won three straight before the Wings won a gut check Game 6. Then, back in Detroit, in the second overtime of a scoreless Game 7, Yzerman delivered a slice of magic (an omen?), a 55-foot slap shot that beat Jon Casey and catapulted the Wings to the conference finals. It was the biggest moment of the Captain's career, more important than we realized at the time.

Think about this. If Yzerman doesn't score that goal, if the Wings don't win that game, everything is altered. If they'd been eliminated in round two, Bowman might not have

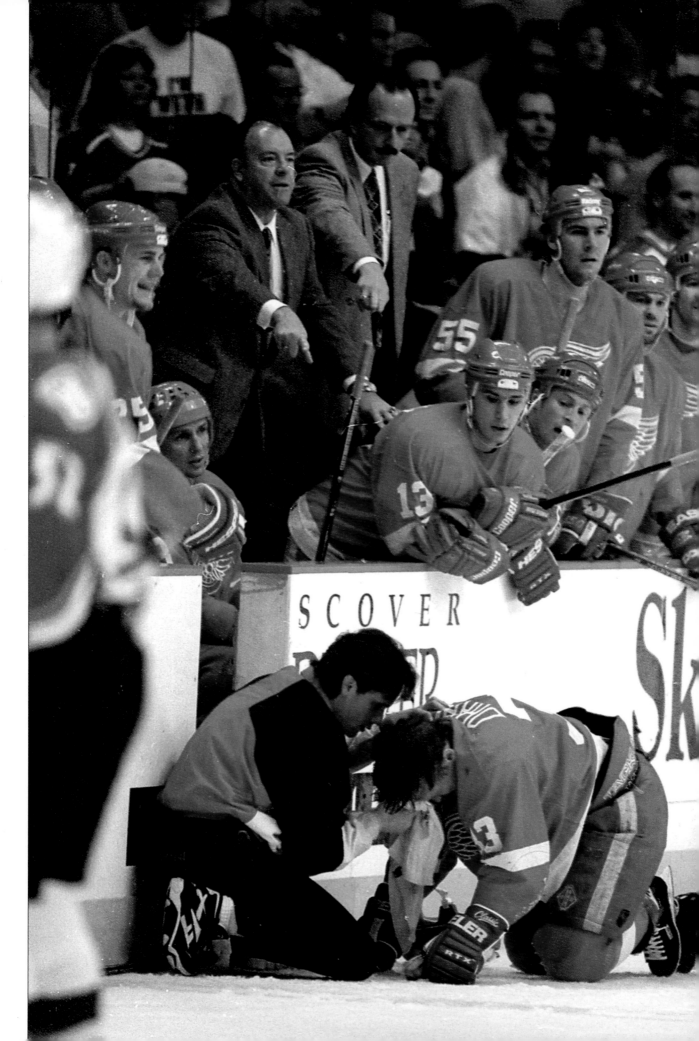

returned. The team might have been shuffled more drastically. And the most relevant lessons never would have been learned from the upcoming opponent, Colorado.

"Everyone dreams of shots like that," said Yzerman, who scored six goals in the series. "We talked about believing in our team. If anything, our will has gotten stronger, our confidence has grown."

From Bowman: "At some point, you have to have adversity."

The Wings had encountered some, apparently not enough. The grind was taking its toll and key players — Primeau, Paul Coffey — were battling injuries. The Avalanche showed up fearing nothing, and who knew it was a look we'd see in the Wings a year later.

Colorado attacked with hunger and size, with the irrepressible Patrick Roy and Claude Lemieux. Their stars — Joe Sakic, Peter Forsberg — played the best hockey of their lives, and in a brutal six-game battle, the Wings lost many of the scrums.

Lemieux caused emotional and physical damage, sucker-punching Vyacheslav Kozlov in one game, then the infamous hit, perhaps the most compelling thing to happen to the Wings in years. He crunched Kris Draper from behind, into the boards, and Draper's bloodied, crushed face was the symbol of the series. It was a wound that became a scar that became a badge that became a promise.

"We'll see him next year, and we're going to make it no secret what we're going to do to him,"

Osgood said. "It's stupid what he did, and it's the last time he's going to get away with it."

The Wings' anger would grow as Lemieux taunted them with jabs such as, "If they're concerned about retaliation for next year, that's a sad way to end a season."

For the Wings, it was the saddest way, their record accomplishments now mocking them. It also was the most important way, for now it was perfectly clear. They'd been fooled by success, lulled into trying again with a smallish team, but with this defeat, they learned more than they ever had, and dug the deepest well of motivation.

"We said all year the only thing that matters is working to be successful in the playoffs, and maybe we lost track of that," Yzerman said. "It's like we should take the regular season off and show up in April. This team wasn't good enough to win the Stanley Cup. Obviously, something has to be done different. We're close, but we're not there. Something has to change."

Finally, the acknowledgement. After the seven-game loss to San Jose, the Wings thought maybe it was a fluke. After the sweep by New Jersey, they figured their trip to the Finals had shaken them, and major changes weren't necessary. But another regular-season masterpiece followed by a playoff flop had convinced them it was time for the third step — Final Refining.

This is the tough one. Many teams reach the level of perennial contenders, few go farther. One

wrong move, one trade that's too risky, or not risky enough, can be the difference.

If the New Jersey series was the primer, Colorado hammered it home. Bowman had gotten caught up in all the sideshows, yelling at Lemieux in a parking lot, griping about the officiating. He was obsessed with how a game was called because he knew the Wings had to draw penalties to score goals.

After Game 6 in Denver ended, the Wings headed home, battered, bloodied ... enlightened. From that moment, everything that happened — brawls, suspensions, trades, words — built to the rematch in 1997, when the Wings could prove how studious they'd been.

In the off-season, Bowman traded Dino Ciccarelli, partly because he was small and getting old, partly because he took bad penalties against the Avalanche. Then, early in the season, Bowman sealed the deal that made it clear the Wings were attacking from a different angle. He traded Primeau and Coffey, playoff underachievers, to Hartford for Brendan Shanahan, acquiring size and spirit.

Later, he added Joe Kocur. He put together the Grind Line of Maltby, Kocur and Draper, and by the end of the season, it was getting as much playing time as the Russian unit. He gave tough rookie defenseman Aaron Ward more ice time.

Most important, Bowman and the Wings finally practiced what they had beseeched — that the regular season means nothing. They coasted to a 38-26-18 record, third in the

Center Kris Draper (33) was pummeled by Colorado's Claude Lemieux in Game 6 of the 1996 Western Conference Finals.

Western Conference. They held back so they could hold up when the games mattered. They watched the attention turn to Colorado, Dallas and Philadelphia, and privately, they relished their new role.

Oh, they had their 1996-97 regular-season moments. There was Bowman's 1,000th victory against Pittsburgh on Feb. 8, when Shanahan asserted himself with a hat trick. There was a 4-1 victory at Philadelphia, the first clue that the Wings could turn it on, when necessary.

The second clue came on March 26, the signature date, when Lemieux and the Avalanche came to town expecting to find the same broken Wings, and discovered things were different. Everything changed that night, the psychology of the rivalry, the dynamics of the season, the psyche of the Wings.

McCarty threw a punch he had spent a year coiling, and when Lemieux hit the ice and assumed the position, the Wings became the dominant team. The only thing left to do was prove it. Vernon fought Roy that game, Shanahan protected McCarty with a flying leap on Roy and the Wings won on an overtime goal by McCarty. The impact of that game cannot be minimized. The demons had been shooed, and free of the psychological baggage, the Wings were able to move forward.

"Maybe this is what we needed," Vernon said. "It shows we're willing to go to war for each other. This was the game that brought the Red Wings together. The boys were willing to pay the price."

By the time the playoffs hit, the Wings were hungrier, healthier, more physical, armed with precious knowledge, the only gift Colorado ever gave them.

They had the intangibles, the extra stride, the deepest well of emotion — revenge. They struggled early against St. Louis, and when the series was tied 2-2, Yzerman stood up in the dressing room and demanded more, starting with himself. It was a tangible sign he was leading, more than ever.

And now, it was the captain, the coach and the goalie. Vernon, given the full-time job because Bowman liked his experience and composure, was magnificent. Fighting for another year on his contract, he helped the Wings sweep Anaheim, winning three games in overtime.

Then came Colorado, which really was the final test, although Philadelphia awaited.

"If you're writing a script on how to get better, you take your last experience and figure out why you didn't advance," McCarty said. "We knew we had to get bigger. We knew we had to play disciplined. It's our job to dethrone them, and we believe we can do it."

They did it with such ferocity, they drove Avalanche coach Marc Crawford up a wall, or at least up a glass partition during Game 5, a 6-0 Detroit victory that featured a third period loaded with brawls. Crawford tried to get at Bowman, who watched with a bemused look, cool and confident, just like his team.

So many people answered so many questions during that series, from Sergei Fedorov and his swift-skating Russian linemates, to Vernon, to grinders such as Martin Lapointe, McCarty and Maltby. The Wings had learned they were too small and too soft, and had brought in nastier players such as Shanahan, Tomas Sandstrom, Larry Murphy, Kocur and Ward to remedy it.

Once they dispatched the Avalanche, there was nothing to stop them. The Flyers became the Wings of 1995, and maybe the cycle begins for them. The cycle ended for the Wings two years after it began in a dank dressing room in New Jersey, where they gathered the information a championship team must collect.

The Wings' sweep of Philadelphia was brutally efficient, and again, they received help from all quarters, all lines. Vernon won the Conn Smythe, but the only trophy that mattered was the big silver one, hoisted by the captain, helped by the goalie, guided by the coach, surrounded by a true team.

"The great thing about this team was, everybody accepted their roles," Yzerman said. "We got goals and contributions from everyone. Everyone did their jobs, no questions asked."

No reason to ask. Questions had been posed for two years, across three seasons. History teaches, failure teaches. Champions learn. The Red Wings took a series of events and experiences and made a map out of them. They followed it from the lowest point to the highest point, where finally, finally, the cheers were all for them.

Vladimir Konstantinov (16) battles with the Flyers' Eric Lindros in 1996.

1996-97
Team of Destiny

COOLEST
GAME
on earth.

A season full of magical moments

By Cynthia Lambert

The Detroit News

D estiny.

It's a quirky word believed by some, scoffed at by others. But if any one word could be used to describe the sentiment of the Red Wings in their first Cup-winning season in 42 years, that would be it.

"We are a team of destiny," Sergei Fedorov said throughout the playoffs.

Yet, when the Red Wings look back on this 1996-97 season, there will be ample material and events to sift through, presenting them with the reasons why it finally worked. As with any team that achieves great success, it is the sum of the parts, not one person or single event that is responsible for seeing the plan through.

But the success of the Wings did start with one obsessed man, who made trades, shifted lines and finally found the mix that worked. All he needed then was for the players to carry it out.

Scotty Bowman, in his fourth season as head coach of the Red Wings, started the 1996-97 season with a big trade to bring Brendan Shanahan to Detroit, a deal that will be viewed as the key.

Bowman had made other trades since taking over as director of player personnel in the summer of 1994.

His first deal was to trade defenseman Steve Chiasson to Calgary for Mike Vernon. The move was one of several key deals Bowman pulled off on the way to collecting the players he wanted for this Red Wings team.

But no trade was as crucial — or as difficult to pull off — than the one he made on Oct. 9 for Shanahan, a power forward the Wings knew they needed for two years. It was the one deal Bowman had to push for, the one he fought to consummate. And in the end, it might have been the deal that finally helped vault the Wings to their historic accomplishment.

"He's the total package," Bowman said of Shanahan, who scored 47 goals in the 1996-97 season.

But to get Shanahan, Bowman first had to convince team senior vice-president Jimmy Devellano that Shanahan was worth acquiring for disgruntled Keith Primeau, who had demanded a trade and was sitting at

home awaiting news, future Hall of Fame defenseman Paul Coffey and a No. 1 draft pick.

Wings captain Steve Yzerman helped the cause by telling Bowman that, from what he had observed during the World Cup of Hockey tournament, Shanahan was the real thing.

"Scotty fought for that trade, he fought it all the way," said Wings associate coach Barry Smith, a long-time friend of Bowman's.

The deal was one that went from on, to off, to back on again, all within a matter of days, and sometimes within hours. Bowman first thought he had the deal done on the morning of the team's season opener, Oct. 5, in New Jersey. He was so certain, he told Coffey to return home and went so far as to tell the defenseman he didn't care how he got there. The comment set off a string of controversy that Coffey refused to become part of, and bowed out of any com-

---

Overleaf: The Red Wings took flight after defeating Patrick Roy and the Avalanche on March 26, 1997.

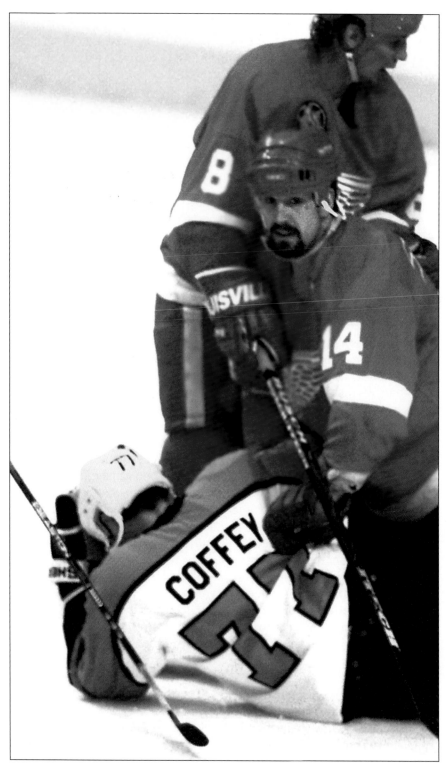

Brendan Shanahan (14), Igor Larionov (8) and the Wings contained former teammate and Flyers defenseman Paul Coffey.

ments. And though the defenseman returned to practicing with the team over the next couple of days, he was told the afternoon of Oct. 9, the day of the Wings' home opener, that he was a member of the Hartford Whalers.

Earlier that day, Shanahan was told his dream job was a reality. He boarded a private jet sent by Wings owner Mike Ilitch and arrived at Joe Louis Arena minutes before the warm-ups started. In a show of unity and acceptance, Yzerman walked over to Shanahan, shook his hand and told him the team would not take the ice until he could go with them. Shanahan dressed hurriedly and skated out for what would be one of many key moments in the Red Wings' season of destiny. And after the game, his words supported the theory that he was just what Detroit needed.

"I am a piece but I don't see myself as a missing piece," Shanahan said. "This is a spectacular team. The important thing is to come to a town with the mandate to win the Stanley Cup. There is pressure from the city and the team puts pressure on itself.

"That's what I want. I like being in the big games, in the big moments. When I heard the fans cheering, I thought, this is the start of it, not the end of it. I welcome it."

The Wings fans welcomed Shanahan with hungry arms. Finally, that big, rugged winger was wearing the winged wheel.

The key dealings might have begun with Shanahan, but they didn't end there. Two other trades further helped Detroit's season come together. One was sending Greg Johnson to Pittsburgh for winger Tomas Sandstrom. The other was trading for Toronto defenseman Larry Murphy.

Not only did the two veteran players bring with them Cup-winning experience, but sizable contracts. Both factors showed again how badly the organization wanted to bring the Cup to Detroit.

"The fans and players, to some degree, felt we needed someone like Brendan, that type of player," defenseman Bob Rouse said. "But when they brought Murphy and Sandstrom here, that was another indication for us, the players. They were two veteran players making decent compensation. It showed the team was willing to do whatever it took to win. Both of those look like great moves now."

Not to be forgotten was Bowman's insistence on signing free agent and former Red Wings enforcer Joe Kocur. After losing Stu Grimson to the waiver wire in October, the team lacked a proven tough guy. And although he had played for the Red Wings Alumni team, a 30-and over beer league in the Detroit area, and finally with the San Antonio Dragons of the International Hockey League in December, Kocur looked as though he had never left the NHL. And ultimately, Kocur played regularly, even logging more ice time in the Finals, to help the checking line click.

All of those moves were made by one man — with the approval of many. They were made to bring the qualities Bowman felt necessary to win in the playoffs.

But Bowman also moved out those players he felt might hinder that process. His tenuous popularity took a serious hit before the season began, when he dispatched Dino Ciccarelli to Tampa Bay for a late-round draft

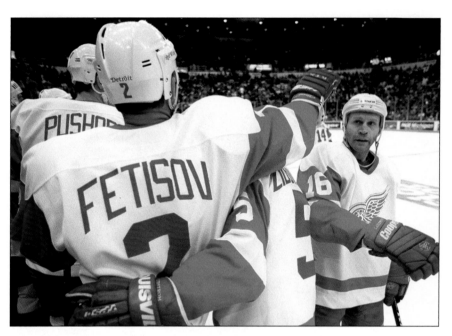

Russians Slava Fetisov and Vladimir Konstantinov (16), and Nicklas Lidstrom (5) helped anchor the Red Wings' defense.

pick, one of the most unpopular trades in recent memory.

"Say what you want about Dino, but the move gave more ice time to guys like Martin Lapointe and Darren McCarty," assistant general manager Ken Holland said. "It was a move that had to be made, to clear the way."

McCarty and Lapointe played key roles in the playoffs, unsettling opponents with their demeanor and startling them with their timely offense. Also leaving the team was forward Bob Errey, another player who was known to question Bowman's reasoning and demands.

What remained was a group determined to play without threat of mutiny. Even Yzerman, who had the credentials and the ability to challenge moves or strategy, kept his mouth shut and went along with Bowman's wishes.

"We're in no position to doubt what the winningest coach in the history of the game wants us to do," Kris Draper said. "I think this year we had to realize the accomplishments he's had. When you think about how he's won 1,000 games. I'm not talking about coaching 1,000 games, but actually winning 1,000. I look at how he's adapted over the years to the times and the players. It takes a lot to do that.

"We lost in the Cup Finals two years ago. But I look around the room in these Finals and everyone who was in this room was here because Scotty wanted them here. This is the team Scotty wanted and look what we were able to do."

But all of Bowman's moves were not for the better. By the end of the regular season, forward Sergei Fedorov — a former Hart Trophy winner as the league's MVP, and winner of the Selke Trophy as the league's best two-way forward — had

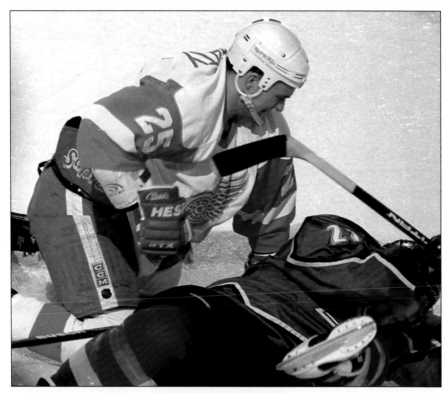

Darren McCarty (25) exacted revenge for his best friend and teammate, Kris Draper, by pummeling the Avalanche's Claude Lemieux.

played every position except goalie. His games on defense were the most challenging for a career forward who fought between keeping his feelings suppressed and venting to the media. The great experiment finally ended early in a first-round playoff series against St. Louis, when Bowman realized he needed to reunite the Russian Five. Once that move was made, Fedorov never returned to defense, and began to flourish up front.

Bowman tried a similar experiment with forward Mathieu Dandenault, playing him on defense and later playing with his mind. Dandenault, Detroit's second pick in the 1994 entry draft, was in the line-up for the first 48 games, but played in only 17 of the next 34. He didn't get

into a single playoff game and was left to wonder if he is a forward or defenseman. He was put in a position that seemed unnecessary and uncalled for.

Bowman also had to adjust to changes of his own. In December, Smith, his top assistant, was offered a head-coaching job in the Swedish Elite League. Smith took it, after being told by the team that if Bowman didn't return to coaching for the 1997-98 season he would not succeed him. Bowman encouraged Smith to take the job, but told him to return to Detroit in March after the Swedish league concluded. Then, before clearing it with upper management, Bowman hired former player Mike Krushelnyski as an assistant

and informed the media that Smith would return for the end of the regular season and the playoffs.

While Bowman worked for control of his staff, the Wings took control of their season in a game more remembered as an event, and one that will forever be remembered as the night the Wings didn't just get even, but pulled ahead.

Until the March 26 game against Colorado, the Wings not only had the playoff proving ground ahead of them, but putting some unfinished business from a May 29, 1996, playoff game in Denver behind them. That was the night the Wings were eliminated from the Western Conference finals, and also the night Claude Lemieux crushed Draper face-first into the boards. Draper sustained multiple facial fractures, displaced teeth and was put through further torture when he was faced with the fact that Lemieux and his Avalanche went on to sweep the Florida Panthers to win the Stanley Cup.

All of it was made worse because of Lemieux's refusal to apologize to Draper, and made unbearable with the Colorado forward's despicable comments regarding Draper's limited talents and how his hit made him a household word.

Every time Lemieux spoke, more fuel was poured on the Detroit fire. Even Shanahan, new to the scene and a friend of Lemieux's, took up the Red Wings' collective cause. Before the March 26 meeting, the first time Lemieux played in Detroit since the incident, Shanahan spoke of how he reveled in the fact that Lemieux was off balance, not knowing if Shanahan was a friend or foe.

"I want him wondering when he gets out there," Shanahan said the morning of the game. "He doesn't know how I feel about him and he won't know until game time."

Shanahan was the first to hit Lemieux in the game, and followed through by dumping him to the ice with a modified cross check. But the real fireworks exploded at 18:22 of the first period, when a seemingly insignificant hit by center Peter Forsberg on Igor Larionov set off a string of events that resulted in Lemieux's pummeling at the hands of McCarty at center ice.

"I don't know how we ended up together," McCarty would say with a smile after the game. "Maybe it was God's will."

Whatever the reason, McCarty took advantage of the situation and thoroughly spent himself on the player who rearranged his best friend's face.

"He looked right at me," McCarty said of Lemieux. "He didn't want any part of me, but he saw me coming. I wanted to make sure of that because I didn't want people thinking I wasn't fair about it."

As McCarty landed punch after punch to Lemieux, Avalanche goaltender Patrick Roy sprinted from his net to come to his teammate's aid. Before Roy could reach the main event, Shanahan charged onto the scene, intercepting Roy with a flying leap.

"We had a little bit of the WWF going there," Shanahan said later.

And as Adam Foote came to Roy's aid, Vernon came out of the Detroit net to even the match-up. The result was a slug-for-slug fight at center ice between Vernon and Roy — an almost humorous match-up with the 5-foot-9, 166-pound Detroit goalie squaring off against Roy, who is 6-0, 192.

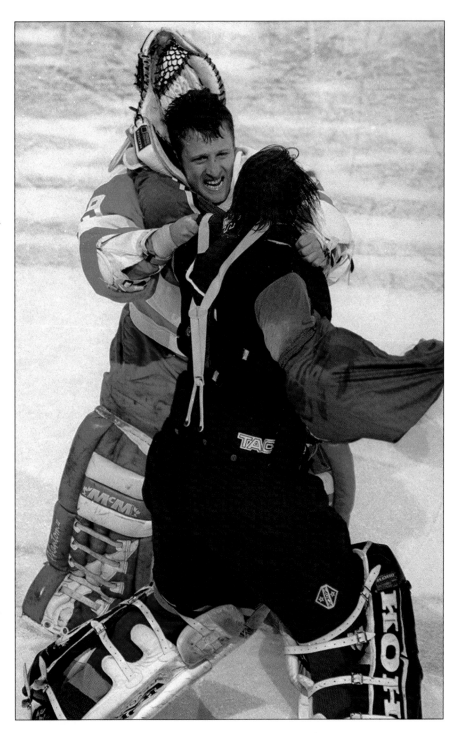

"I did what anyone else in my position would have done," Vernon said.

Following the game — a 6-5 Detroit victory — Avalanche center Mike Keane labeled the Wings as gutless and heartless for not confronting Lemieux when the teams played 10

In an undercard to the March 26 slugfest, Wings' Mike Vernon squared off against Patrick Roy, leaving the Avalanche goalie worse for wear.

days earlier in Denver. They were comments that would continue to fuel the Wings throughout the season. And later, when the teams met in the Western Conference finals, they would haunt Keane.

But more significantly, that March 26 game gave the Wings a sense of closure for the previous season and opened up a new set of possibilities for what might lie ahead in the upcoming months. As ruthless and bloody as the night became, it showed to each Detroit player and to other clubs observing, that the Wings were a team, in every sense of the word.

"A game like this can help the confidence of the team and bring the guys together even more," Vernon said. "It was a good game all around. We made a lot of things happen. I don't think there's any question that it is the game that brought this team together."

That sense of unity was tested early in the playoffs, as the Wings struggled to manufacture offense and maintain momentum against the St. Louis Blues. The series started with Grant Fuhr stifling the Wings at Joe Louis Arena, 2-0. Detroit came back to win the next two games, but lost Game 4, 4-0, in St. Louis. The series was tied at two games apiece, and Game 5 was at Joe Louis Arena.

"Game 5 of the St. Louis series was when we showed we have a real team in this dressing room," defenseman

Slava Fetisov said. "In that game we didn't depend on one or two guys. All four lines worked hard and contributed.

Detroit won Game 5, 5-2, a contest highlighted by the reuniting of the Russian Five. The Wings won Game 6, and the series, 3-1, on goals by Vyacheslav Kozlov, Shanahan and Kirk Maltby.

It would be the closest the Wings would feel to being eliminated in the playoffs. Their next round, against the Mighty Ducks of Anaheim, would be a sweep.

Three of the four games went into overtime, including triple overtime in Game 2. The clincher went 17:03 into the second overtime before Shanahan scored the winner. And as many of the players believed, Detroit's season of destiny showed itself through an interesting statistic that would ultimately test the Wings' patience.

"We kept saying that we played more overtime games than any other team," Shanahan said. "I think that was good preparation for this."

If the Wings learned discipline in the series against the Blues and patience against the Ducks, their overall mettle was pushed to its extreme in the rematch with the Avalanche in the Western Conference final.

Vernon, who had been strong in net until this point, was considered the weak link for Detroit compared to Roy's dominance in the playoffs for the Avalanche. Goaltending would be the key, it was predicted. How true. But it was Vernon who outshone Roy to put the Wings in the Cup Finals for the second time in three seasons after winning the series, 4-2.

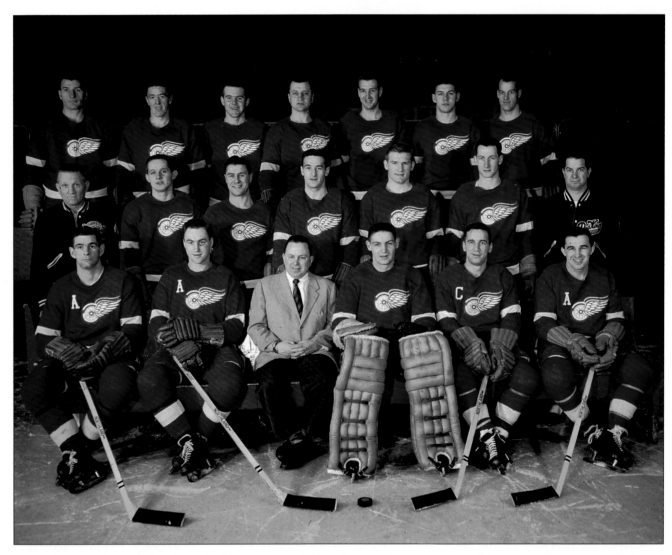

Front row, left to right: Bob Goldham, Len Kelly, James Skinner (coach), Terry Sawchuk, Ted Lindsay, Marty Pavelich. Second row: Carl Mattson (trainer), Earl Reibel, Tony Leswick, Marcel Bonin, John Wilson, Bill Dineen, Lefty Wilson (assistant trainer). Third row: Vic Stasiuk, Marcel Pronovost, Jim Hay, Benny Woit, Glen Skov, Alex Delvecchio and Gordie Howe.

Times have changed since Cup's last visit

By Joe Falls

The Detroit News

IMAGINE THIS: DARREN MCCARTY AND CLAUDE LEMIEUX GOING INTO the same penalty box and sitting next to each other, separated only by a stadium guard. Or maybe an usher.

Mayhem.

They would have to paint the penalty box red to hide the blood.

But that's how it was in Olympia Stadium in 1955 — when the Red Wings won the Stanley Cup.

A lot of things were different 42 years ago. None of these modern-day Red Wings was even born, and Scotty Bowman was 22 years old and had not even thought about coaching. He was trying to think of ways to pay his grocery bill.

The Production Line: From left, Gordie Howe, Sid Abel and Ted Lindsay.

It was a simple time in many ways. World War II was over for 10 years and the country was at peace. We were in the middle of the Dwight D. Eisenhower presidency and the main thrust was to buy a home, buy a car and begin raising your children.

Some have called it one of the most tranquil periods in our history. Nothing much was going on except living quiet, peaceful lives.

Only a few of us had television sets. Drugs were something you got at the drug stores. Drive-in theaters were big, and frozen vegetables were starting to appear in markets.

The year 1955 was a time when: Jazz saxophonist Charley Parker died, Winston Churchill retired as Prime Minister of Great Britain, *Cat on a Hot Tin Roof* opened on Broadway, Bill Vukovich died trying for his third straight Indy 500 victory, former Argentina president Juan Peron was ousted, painter Grandma Moses turned 95, President Eisenhower had a heart attack, the Brooklyn Dodgers won their first World Series, 24-year-old actor James Dean died when his Porsche Spider crashed, the *Mickey Mouse Club and the Mouseketeers* debuted on TV, Cy Young died and *Damn Yankees* became the theater hit of the year.

We were just starting to pick up *Hockey Night in Canada* on Saturday nights (first, the weekly bath, then Foster Hewitt from the Gondola in Maple Leaf Gardens.) We were never sure what the Gondola was, but it hung high over The Gardens and it seemed like the most wonderful place in the world.

How could somebody be so lucky to work in a Gondola. It was Hewitt's broadcast booth and we got the same thrill every Saturday night when he began the show: "Hello, Canada. It is clear and cold in Toronto and we're talking to you from the Gondola high in Maple Leafs Gardens."

And, of course, it was Murray Westgate with that mechanic's cap, pleasant smile and neat, gray hair who sold us our gas and oil, just before those sports writers and broadcasters started in with their "Hot Stove League" between the periods. (I always thought they had a hot stove hidden somewhere in the studio, but I never did see it).

And then, what we all waited for: Hewitt's favorite call — "He shoots, he scores!" Maybe it wasn't as glamorous as Maple Leaf Gardens, but Olympia Stadium in Detroit wasn't bad.

They had Apps, Drillon, Broda, Kennedy, Ezinicki and Hewitt; we had Abel, Lindsay, Howe, Kelly, Delvecchio, Pronovost and Al Nagler. I always wished Nagler would stop calling Vic Stas-IUK, Vic Stas-IAK. But he never did.

How those penalty boxes remained standing was, in retrospect, rather amazing. We just didn't know any better. We didn't even have Zambonis in those days, just four guys pushing two tanks of water around the ice between periods to smooth things out. We always told ourselves it was hot water because hot water would freeze quicker than cold water. That didn't make any sense but that's what someone said and it was a nice thing to know. You'd tell one of your buddies that the water was hot — "Look at the way it steams" — and this gave you an edge on him because he didn't know one way or the other.

Hey, there were a lot of things we didn't know in 1955. We had never heard of Brigitte Bardot, Sputnik, slap shots, crack, Dealy Plaza, Ali, the Beatles, Watts, Johnny Carson, Martin Luther King, Chappaquiddick, Kent State, Saigon, *Jaws*, Beirut, *Taxi Driver*, HIV, "Make my day," Jonestown, "One small step for man ...," Margaret Thatcher, Mother Teresa, the Wall crumbles, Super Bowl, Blues Brothers, Chris Osgood, Ted Turner, Nelson Mandella, skud missiles, John Gotti, *Rain Man*, *Les Miz*, Chernobyl, CNN, Tiananmen Square, E-Mail.

Did I tell you about the night Mr. Lindsay met Mr. Bill Ezinicki in our penalty box?

Most of the times the guys behaved themselves in there. They learned to cool off and, besides, they didn't want the guards or ushers to get hurt. They didn't make much money and didn't need this kind of grief.

Lindsay and Ezinicki got into a stick duel on the ice and were sent off for two minutes. A lot of words and some pushing and shoving took place in the penalty box, with a few swings over the head and behind the back of the poor guy sitting between them.

When their penalties expired, they stepped on the ice and went right at each other. Ezinicki swung his stick and hit Lindsay on the shoulder. Lindsay swung his stick and missed. That was the last time he missed.

Lindsay started swinging his fists and landed about 10 straight blows. Ezinicki didn't get off so much as a punch. He finally fell face first to the ice, with Lindsay falling on him and pounding the back of his head. Ezinicki's blood started staining the ice.

The officials looked on almost indifferently, as if to say: "Well, it's just those two — let them go."

It was not a pleasant sight but that's how it went between these two men. A pair of ruffians, they hated each other. One wore the Blue and White of the Maple Leafs, the other the winged wheel of the Red Wings.

That was more than enough for a little mayhem. There weren't too many teams to hate in those days — just six.

The 1954-55 season was the first time teams began using backup goalies. If a goalie got hurt, well, the trainer or one of the other players would take over. A strange tactic that would not be allowed in today's big-money matches. But it was romantic at the time and no one ever questioned such strategy.

That season probably marked Gordie Howe's worst scoring slump in the NHL. He started fast with 20 goals in his first 37 games, but got just four over the next 17..

In November, Lindsay scored his 250th career goal. After playing five big seasons in the Detroit nets, Terry Sawchuk was replaced, without consultation, when General Manager Jack Adams and Coach Jimmy Skinner felt the strain of goaltending was affecting Sawchuk's work. Sawchuk was high-strung, often blowing up for no reason, and he brooded a lot when there didn't seem much to brood about.

Sawchuk was back after a few games and went on to win the Vezina Trophy as the league's No. 1 goalie.

On Jan. 22, Lindsay was given a 10-day suspension for striking a spectator with his stick in a game in Toronto. The incident occurred after Eric Nesterenko of the Leafs and Howe scuffled along the boards and the fan grabbed Howe's stick. As Howe pulled away, the fan reached over the boards to hit him. Lindsay, who was 30 or 40 feet away, rushed forward and struck the fan.

Actually, the fans were very calm in those days.

"When you played in Maple Leaf Gardens, it seemed like going to an opera," Lindsay said. "The people in the box red seats — now gold — were dressed like it was a formal affair. Suits, ties — even tuxedos. They made you feel you were undressed, even in your uniform.

"Anyone who acted up, like throwing something on the ice, was given a notice by the Maple Leafs' management. Even if they were season-ticket holders, some would have their tickets picked up."

In Detroit, there were no tuxedos. But the fans were well dressed — shirts, ties, jackets, with the women in some of their finest evening wear. The fans loved their hockey, even the violence, but always remained detached from the scene. They behaved themselves and did not try to become part of the show.

What was it like in Olympia Stadium?

The arena was located on Grand River and McGraw, just south of Grand Boulevard and next to Northwestern High School. It was about five miles from downtown Detroit.

Part of the excitement of going to a game was the traffic on Grand River. It was always horrendous, but a major part of the experience. You knew the jam-up would be there — more impossible than ever — and you tried to figure out small ways to get two cars ahead, or slip in front of the car next to you.

We all did it.

Once you could see the marquee blazing outside the arena (Tonight: Detroit vs. Boston), you could feel the adrenaline start running. You were getting close, but not that close. You would move 10 feet, then stop. Five feet, then stop.

What complicated matters is that the fans used to park in all kinds of places around Olympia Stadium — on the streets, in small lots, in alleys and even on front lawns, which were very small and could accommodate only a few cars. These would make the rest of the journey on foot, scrambling across Grand River by cutting between the cars, sometimes climbing over your hood if you were too close to the car in front, but again, you didn't mind. This was Hockey Night in Detroit.

The press lot was just beyond the traffic jam in front of Olympia Stadium and it was always with a sigh of relief when the guard waved you in to the right. You did it with much trepidation, though, because you knew the fans hurrying through the cold night air would start in on you when they saw the preferential treatment you were getting.

They would yell all kinds of things:

"Big man! Big car! Big deal!"

"Hey, creep, pay your way!"

Or, if they recognized you: "Hey, Falls, good stuff lately. Who has been writing it for you?"

I used to wear a baseball cap and pull it down over my eyes. It didn't help.

The stadium, as I recall, seated a little more than 14,000. It had a balcony, which made it a real hockey rink, and the seats up high were only a couple of bucks.

The press box was just under the balcony and we were so close to the ice we could see Gordie Howe's eyes blinking from an injury he suffered

Gordie Howe, right, was more than just a goal scorer ... he could also throw some vicious checks.

when he collided with Ted Kennedy in the playoffs a few years earlier.

I worked for The Associated Press in those days and my seat was between Marshall Dann, the hockey writer for The Detroit Free Press, and Ross Jewell, the official scorer. Fred Huber, the Wings' erudite publicity man — he could do The New York Times crossword puzzle non-stop in ink — sat next to the official scorer.

Ross Jewell was a very nervous man. He even occasionally stuttered when he spoke. He would sit there,

almost terrified, watching the play. He didn't want to miss a play because a missed play meant criticism from somewhere. He was not up to criticism.

So he would follow the puck carefully and write down the numbers of the players as they touched the puck. If someone scored, he would simply back the numbers up two and give out the assists.

Even then, he was never sure of himself, and when a goal would go in quickly, or from a pileup, he would turn

around in panic and say: "What happened on that one?"

No replays, remember.

I never said anything. Neither did Dann. Huber, ever the intellect — there was nothing he didn't know — would ponder the question for a moment and say: "I can't be absolutely sure, but I think Gordie got the tip of his stick on the puck in the corner."

So, Howe was getting assists he didn't earn, or didn't need. A story like this today would be page-one headlines.

But then, this was 1955.

It was dangerous going into the Red Wings' dressing room. Sawchuk might be in one of his moods and any question could produce a tirade of profanity. All the other players were easy to talk to and they would kind of wink at you as you approached Sawchuk's locker.

In other words: "Not tonight. Stay away."

The room would be strewn with orange slices. Some of these the players ate. Some were thrown at them between periods by Adams. Jolly Jack had a way of getting his message across, by the way he would carry train tickets to Indianapolis in his vest pocket — the city where the Red Wings' farm club played — and they were there for all to see.

The Wings used to play exhibition games against Michigan in Ann Arbor and Michigan State in East Lansing as a way to promote hockey. One time,

Olympia Stadium was home to large crowds, winning hockey and a family atmosphere.

they nearly lost to Michigan. Adams was furious. The moment the team entered the dressing room, he began shouting at a player named Al Dewsbury.

"Nobody ever plays that way for the Detroit Red Wings!" Adams said. "Nobody ever embarrasses this team that way!"

He threw a train ticket at Dewsbury's feet and stormed out of the dressing room. The young man was never heard from again.

Olympia Stadium had a family-type atmosphere. The fans would come in early and stand in the back lobby and greet the players as they came in from the parking lot. Fathers. Mothers. Grandfathers. Grandmothers. And children.

No one asked for autographs. Maybe a few children did, but it was never much of a deal. They all grew to know each other on a first-name basis.

It was the same after the games. The fans would gather in the back lobby to say goodnight to the players, and what was noticable is that players never left quickly, even though their own families might be waiting for them.

They were happy to hang around and chat with the fans. Then, it was on to Chuck Joseph's restaurant on Grand River for a steak and a few beers. Oddly enough, the fans did not follow them there. They knew their place. They were glad to spend some time with the players at the stadium; now it was time to leave them alone.

Another dangerous thing about going into the Red Wings dressing room in those days was trying to interview Howe. He was usually the story of the night and so you had to interview him most of the time.

Be careful, my friend.

He did not like talking about himself.

You would walk up to his locker and he would lean on you with those massive shoulders and pin you against the wall. It hurt, but not so much you couldn't stand it. He had learned how to apply the right pressure for each writer who came around.

You are not about to say much when you are fighting for your breath.

I always wore my overcoat into the dressing room, hoping to absorb some of the pain, but it never really worked.

"Get off me, you big oaf. When are you going to grow up?"

Howe would smile at you. No, make that a leer. He was great at leering.

Once he let you off the wall, he would throw an elbow into your ribs. You knew it was coming but could do nothing about it. He did it so quickly, again administering a dose of pain but nothing you couldn't stand.

Then — and I'll never know how he learned to be so adept — he would reach out and grab the tip of your privates through your pants and give it a little squeeze. That was it — the sign that there would be no interview on this evening. So, you would walk across the room, trying to keep your dignity, in search of someone less provocative, less physical, like maybe Red Kelly, who would almost blush anytime you tried to interview him.

No. 9, of course, was grinning by now. Another one in the victory column.

It was easy interviewing Lindsay. He always had something to say — and he always had the look of an imp in his eye, as if he had just stolen something, but you would never know what it was. You were never sure if you were getting the straight dope from Lindsay,

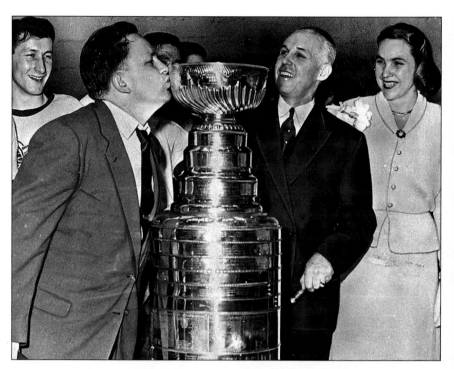

Bill Dineen, Coach Jimmy Skinner (kissing Cup), NHL president Clarence Campbell and Marge Norris celebrate the 1955 title.

but with those scars all over his face, you knew he had earned the right to tell you whatever he wanted. Besides, that crooked smile always took you in. They were really terrific guys in those days — great players and great gentlemen.

Detroit met Toronto in the semifinals in 1955 and won in four straight. The Leafs were without Tim Horton, their great defenseman, and they didn't have much of a power play and the Wings had no trouble handling them.

The Wings and Canadiens went seven games in the finals — rough, fast and without any overtimes. The Wings were in the closing stages of winning seven straight league titles and four Stanley Cups in seven years. Montreal was about to embark on its great run of five straight Stanley Cups with a team many still call the best ever.

Montreal lost the first two games in Olympia Stadium but won the next two in the Montreal Forum. It was in this series that the Canadiens ended a 15-game winning streak by Detroit.

With two goals in the final game, Alex Delvecchio was the hero in the Wings' Cup-clinching victory.

And what was the reaction in Detroit?

Not much.

Everyone had grown accustomed to the Red Wings winning, so it was no big deal. In The Detroit News the next day, the story got third play on the sports page.

It was the opening day of the baseball season and the Tigers dominated the sports pages. The hockey story, written by Harry Stapler, barely made it above the fold of the sports section front. A baseball picture was played over the hockey picture. And there was just one other hockey story, buried inside the section.

Bill Cusimano, the man who threw the first octopus a few years earlier, remembers the night the Red Wings won it all in 1955. He was a friend of Delvecchio and asked if he could have his stick when the game was over.

When it ended, Delvecchio skated to the sideboards and tried to hand his stick to Cusimano. Several fans grabbed for it. Delvecchio pulled it back and finally worked it to his friend.

"I had a treasure and didn't know it," Cusimano said. "I had the stick which scored two goals and won the Stanley Cup. So what did I do with it. I used it in our Belle Isle games on Sunday and when we used to rent the Windsor Arena for 40 bucks an hour at five o'clock in the morning. I busted it.

"Just think what that stick would be worth today. Not in money but in history. I hope Alex never reads this book."

Adams was a man who liked to party. If the Red Wings were in Boston, he thought nothing of taking the entire press delegation to dinner at LockObers — one of the fine eating establishments on the East Coast.

When the Red Wings won Cups in 1954 and 1955, he invited the press (which was comprised mostly of writers) to a party at Yeaman, s nightclub on Howard Street in downtown Detroit. My wife and I drank from the Stanley Cup and danced until dawn.

She was thrilled with my new job.

"How often do they have these parties?" she said.

And I said: "Every year, my dear. Every year."

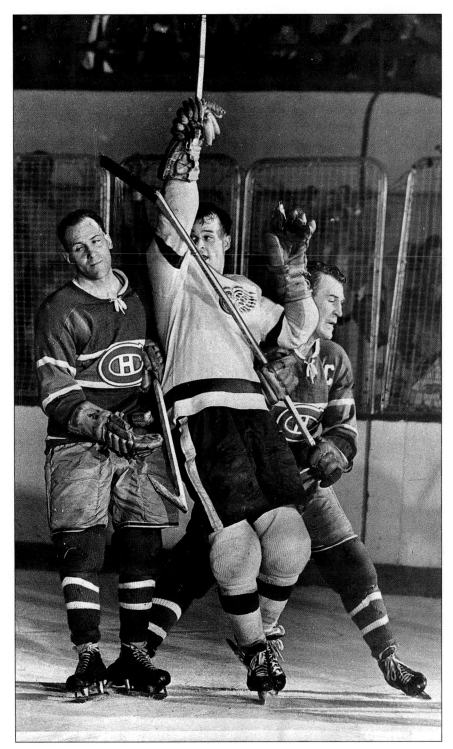

Gordie Howe celebrates his second goal during the Wings' 3-1 victory in the clinching game of the 1955 Stanley Cup Finals.

THE FINALS

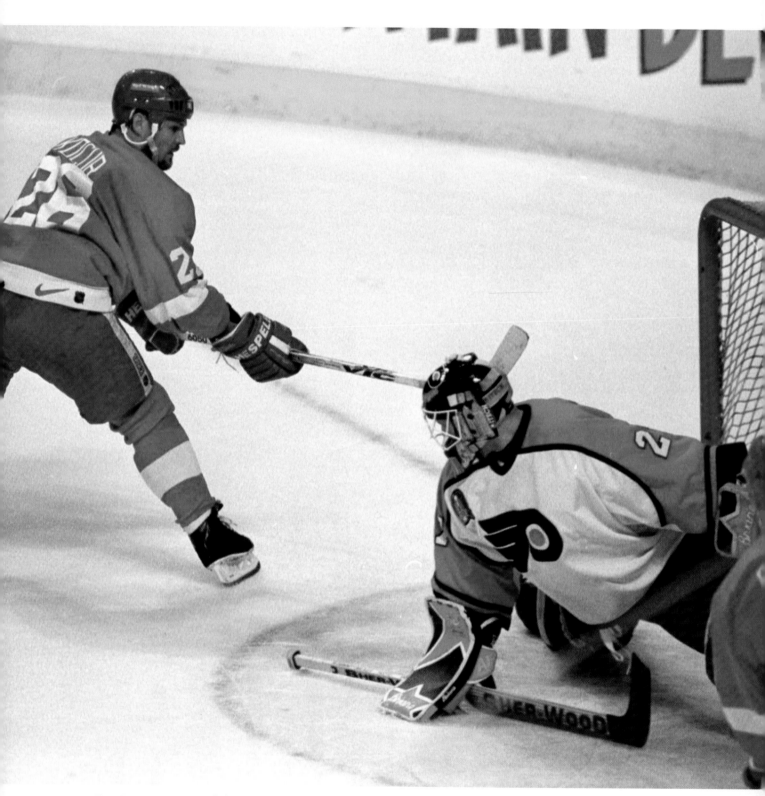

Joe Kocur, part of the Red Wings' Grind Line, beats Ron Hextall in the first period.

WINGS SOLVE HEX

First Finals win since 1966

BY CYNTHIA LAMBERT

The Detroit News

THE RED WINGS CHASED ONE MORE GHOST from their past on Saturday night, when they defeated the Philadelphia Flyers, 4-2, in Game 1 of the Stanley Cup Finals.

The Detroit franchise won for the first in the Finals since it defeated the Montreal Canadiens on April 26, 1966. That victory gave the Wings a 2-0 series lead, but they ended up losing in six games.

"It's great to win one game," associate coach Dave Lewis said. "Nobody talked about it much, but ... this means a lot to the guys."

GAME 1

Red Wings

4

Flyers

2

at Philly
May 31, 1997

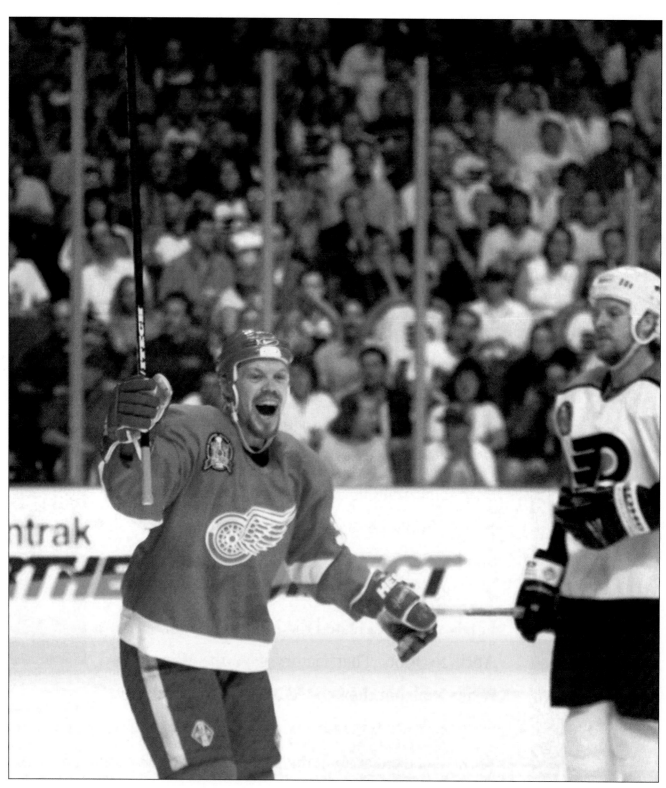

Kris Draper and the Red Wings struck early against the stunned Flyers in Game 1.

The last time the Wings made it this far, they were chased away in four straight by the New Jersey Devils. Since then, the Wings have been waiting to avenge the disgrace. Saturday's victory gave them a start.

"I think it's a huge pat on the back for us," said Mike Vernon, who turned aside 26 shots. "In our series vs. New Jersey, we were very disappointed and embarrassed by what happened. I can look back now and see that we were beat in every area of the game, not just in goals, but in shots and everything. But we learned a valuable lesson from the Devils, and we bring that into this series."

Of course, after a poor showing in Game 1, the Flyers also have motivation from a negative experience.

"We didn't skate well, we didn't support the puck well," captain Eric Lindros said. "We knew what they were going to do, and we didn't do what we had to do to counter that."

Instead, the Flyers tried to rely heavily on their size, a plan for which the Wings prepared.

"They're a physical hockey club," Kris Draper said. "I don't know if we outsmarted them as much as outskated them. I know that's something that I have to do, since most of their guys have 40 or 50 pounds on me. That's my asset."

But scouting also was a Wings asset. Entering the series, they knew the Flyers were vulnerable to defensive lapses. The Wings took advantage of many of those, and exposed Ron Hextall as a goalie they could easily beat — at least on this night.

Hextall gave up first-period goals to Kirk Maltby — the culmination of a two-on-none with Kris Draper — and Joe Kocur, and a second-period goal on a long wrist shot by Sergei

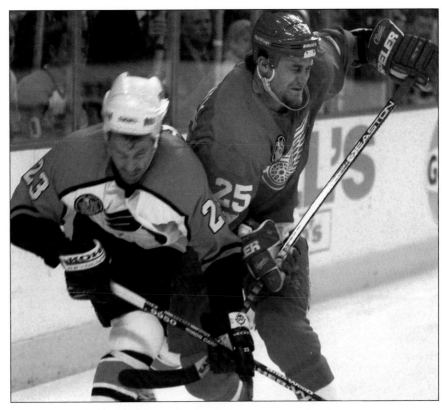

The Flyers' Petr Svoboda (23) and the Wings' Darren McCarty (25) clash during the first period.

Fedorov. But his biggest mistake came on Steve Yzerman's slap shot from the blue line 56 seconds into the third.

The timing of Yzerman's goal was crucial, since it came so quickly into the final period, when the Flyers had to come out strong.

Vernon preserved the Wings' lead late in the third when he made his best save of the game, on Trent Klatt at 14:22. Klatt, at the right circle, took a pass from Lindros and fired a shot at Vernon. He came out of the net to cut the angle.

"What made that save easier is that Vladimir (Konstantinov) and Stevie (Yzerman) came back to take the pass back away," Vernon said. "I thought Klatt might try to go back to Lindros, but they covered that. I came out and

got my glove on the puck."

Rod Brind'Amour (power play) and John LeClair scored for the Flyers. Brind'Amour's came in the first period, and at first it appeared as if Yzerman had scored inadvertently. But Yzerman said Brind'Amour had extended his stick to tap the puck past Vernon during a flurry in front of the net.

LeClair scored late in the second to trim the Wings' lead to 3-2 entering the third. But Yzerman's goal distanced the Flyers again.

The Flyers were never able to try to pull Hextall from the net for the extra attacker. Lindros took a frustration penalty at 17:48 when he slugged Konstantinov in the face, basically sending the Wings on the power play for the rest of the game.

Flyers goalie Ron Hextall was left frazzled after Game I.

Wings unafraid of Flyers

BY BOB WOJNOWSKI

The Detroit News

So, who's afraid of the big, nasty Flyers? If that was the first question of the Stanley Cup Finals — and really, it was — the Red Wings provided the first definitive answer: Not us.

Not the Wings' bashing Grind Line, which added offense to its chores. Not goalie Mike Vernon, who stood up as the Flyers crowded his crease and stormed his net. This was billed as Philadelphia's hulking Legion of Doom, led by Eric Lindros, against the Wings' speedy Masters of Vroom. The Flyers tried to rile the Wings, to knock them off thepuck and off their game, but they wouldn't fluster.

So chalk up Detroit's 4-2 victory in Game One Saturday night to poise and punch, for maintaining the former and avoiding the latter. The Wings have proven they're capable of playing any foe, any style. The Flyers and their frazzled goalie, Ron Hextall, just got their first lesson.

"We're going to do what we can, take the hits and give as many as we

Game One: Where the Wings shot from

● Goal   ● Shot

The Red Wings outshot the Flyers, 30-28, but both teams had plenty of good scoring opportunities. Here is a breakdown of the Wings' individual shots:

No.	Player	Shots
2	Slava Fetisov	1
5	Nicklas Lidstrom	4
13	Vyacheslav Kozlov	1
14	Brendan Shanahan	4
16	Vladimir Konstantinov	1
17	Doug Brown	1
18	Kirk Maltby	2
19	Steve Yzerman	3
20	Martin Lapointe	1
25	Darren McCarty	1
26	Joe Kocur	3
28	Tomas Sandstrom	1
55	Larry Murphy	2
91	Sergei Fedorov	5

Period 1

Period 2

Period 3

can," said Joey Kocur, who scored his first goal of the playoffs. "Our game plan is to get on them as quickly as possible and slow them down, and that's what we did."

While the Flyers played sloppily and even a bit timid, the Wings again showed the maturity they used to lack. This was a game of mistakes — Philadelphia's weak defense made the most miscues, Hextall made the most glaring. Just when the Flyers seemed capable of turning dangerous, captain Steve Yzerman whistled a slapshot from the blue line 56 seconds into the third period, beating a befuddled Hextall cleanly for the goal that sealed the victory.

The Flyers' final act of frustration came with 2:12 left, when Lindros speared and slugged Vladimir Konstantinov, drawing a penalty that effectively killed any comeback.

It was the Grind Line of Kocur, Kirk Maltby and Kris Draper that set the tone. They opened the game against Lindros' line and didn't back off, not for a single shift. Kocur, who was playing in a 30-and-over beer league in December before convincing the Wings he still had NHL value, tried a different shot and chaser this time. He stole an errant pass by Kjell Samuelsson and beat Hextall with a fancy backhander late in the first period, providing a 2-1 lead the Wings never relinquished.

Earlier, Maltby and Draper had netted the first goal on a pretty passing play that ended with Maltby firing the puck over Hextall's shoulder. Now, if you're the Flyers, this is what you're thinking: Kocur? ... Maltby? ... Uh-oh.

"That was important, it gave us a chance to take the pressure off the big guys," Draper said. "We get those two guys scoring and it incites the team."

Really, this is the hidden strength of the Wings, their ability to attack with four lines, four different ways. Sergei Fedorov scored the third goal on a two-on-one, surprising Hextall with a quick slapper. It was the outside game (Fedorov and Yzerman) and the inside game (Kocur, Maltby, Draper), and the Flyers were too busy trying to hit somebody to know what hit them.

The Wings had waited two years to redeem their humbling sweep at the hands of New Jersey in the 1995 finals, and they arrived Saturday night looking like they'd spent their time wisely, building confidence, practicing poise.

They also seemed to skate more freely, and maybe it's because they aren't lugging the old favorite's role.

The Wings are underdogs — "HUGE underdogs" Scotty Bowman said earlier, with a smirk — and frankly, they don't mind. Every writer in both Philadelphia newspapers picked the Flyers to win the series, even after the Wings had vanquished defending champion Colorado with relative ease. There even were TV reports of parade preparations.

"That's the difference between this year and previous years," Maltby said. "There isn't the same pressure on us. It makes it easier to perform."

These Wings look like a team that has traveled this path before. They used to grip their sticks so

Mike Vernon continued his strong playoff play in Game 1.

tightly, they got splinters. But Yzerman keeps spouting the mantra — "Relax" — and Philadelphia could have used the advice.

The Flyers played skittish, while trying desperately to establish the physical game they brag about. They went hunting for big hits while the Wings went hunting for turnovers, and found their prize more often. The Flyers crashed the net with impunity, planting

Lindros in front of Vernon and daring anyone to move him.

But the Wings won because the Flyers turned it over repeatedly, and Detroit's role guys were able to capitalize. When the Grind Line scored twice, the message was clear: The Flyers will be punished for mistakes.

So they were, again and again. Three more games like this and the Wings will have answered everything.

WINGS' CUP HALF FULL

Shanahan Puts Philadelphia in Double Trouble

BY CYNTHIA LAMBERT

The Detroit News

THE RED WINGS PLAYED THEIR WAY into superb position Tuesday night, defeating the Philadelphia Flyers, 4-2, at the CoreStates Center to take a two-games-to-none lead in the best-of-seven Stanley Cup Finals.

The Wings return to Joe Louis Arena for games 3 and 4 on Thursday and Saturday with the odds of winning the series in their favor. Only three times since 1939 have teams rallied from a 2-0 deficit to win a Finals series, and only twice has a team lost the first two at home and won the series.

"We know the position we're in," defenseman Bob Rouse said. "We realize now we're that much closer and that we've put ourselves in a good position. But there's a lot of fight left

Garth Snow and the Flyers are looking up at Brendan Shanahan, left, and Martin Lapointe after Game 2.

GAME 2

Red Wings   Flyers

4   2

at Philly June 3, 1997

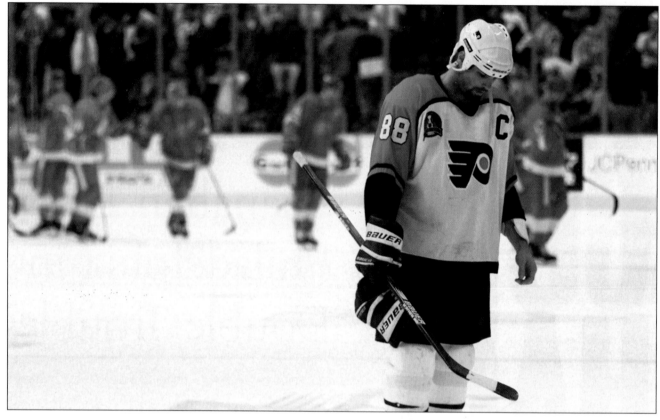

Skating off home ice trailing two games to none was not the way Flyers captain Eric Lindros, above, envisioned things.

in the Flyers and we know that, too."

The Wings also know what the Flyers are up against. In 1995, the Wings lost the first two games at home to the New Jersey Devils in the Finals, and were swept.

"The hunger level for us elevates now," said Brendan Shanahan, who scored twice. "We know winning on the road doesn't mean anything unless you can do it at home, too. There's a lot of hockey left in front of us yet."

Not if Philadelphia can't find better goaltending.

As in Game 1, soft goals allowed by the Flyers helped the Wings win. In Game 2, Garth Snow — not Ron Hextall — was the culprit.

"We have to have a higher responsibility to ... play better and it starts with the goaltender," Flyers coach Terry Murray said. "We had too many breakdowns and too many turnovers. That, and not getting big stops, are the biggest nightmare for a team in the Stanley Cup Finals."

Goaltending also was the story for the Wings. Mike Vernon was outstanding, making big saves throughout.

"I don't know what the perception is out there," Wings defenseman Larry Murphy said. "But anybody in this room definitely hasn't overlooked Mike and what he's done for us. The guys in here are thankful for him being there. In the room after the first two games,

everyone's come in and gone over and patted Mike on the back because we know what he's done for us."

Coach Scotty Bowman said Vernon was a key against the Flyers.

"He's an experienced goalie and the Flyers get a lot of people in front because of their size," Bowman said. "So for him it's a case of knowing when to cover the bottom of the net or when to freeze the puck. He's handling the puck very well in this series, and that has helped our defensemen because I thought tonight their shootins were better than they were in the first game."

Vernon, who is 14-4 in the playoffs this year, said he is playing the game he has always played.

"I'm just trying to get myself in good position," he said. "I'm not the type of goaltender to come way out of the net. I'm just trying to hold my ground."

Steve Yzerman had a power-play goal and Kirk Maltby also scored for the Wings. Shanahan's first goal and Maltby's were on shots from beyond the top of the faceoff circles.

Detroit led, 3-2, after two periods, and made it 4-2 thanks to a breakdown in the Philadelphia defense. The Wings got a two-on-one break, with Paul Coffey as the only Flyer back. Martin Lapointe, closing on the right, passed to Shanahan, whose shot from the left dot beat Snow.

Rod Brind'Amour scored two power-play goals on high deflections. But the goals weren't enough to offset a poor performance by Snow, who started after Hextall's subpar performance in Game 1.

"It seems like we're always chasing from behind," Flyers forward Mikael Renberg said. "That's a tough way to play."

Had the Flyers received better goaltending from Snow, the outcome might have been different. Unlike Game 1, the Flyers used their speed and were successful at dumping the puck in the Wings' zone and keeping it there with strong forechecking.

The Flyers' speed was boosted by lineup changes, and they tied the score despite the Wings taking a 2-0 lead by 9:22 of the first period.

"They did a few adjustments in the first half of the game," Bowman said. "I thought they made shorter passes. They had more speed through the neutral zone and we got trapped a few times. But I think we adjusted. We did

Game 2: Where the Wings shot from

● Goal   ● Shot

For the second time in the playoffs, the Wings were outshot by their opponent.

No.	Player	Shots
2	Slava Fetisov	1
3	Bob Rouse	2
5	Nicklas Lidstrom	2
8	Igor Larionov	1
13	Vyacheslav Kozlov	1
14	Brendan Shanahan	5
16	Vladimir Konstantinov	1
17	Doug Brown	1
18	Kirk Maltby	2
19	Steve Yzerman	4
20	Martin Lapointe	3
26	Joe Kocur	1
28	Tomas Sandstrom	1
33	Kris Draper	1
91	Sergei Fedorov	2

Shanny time

Brendan Shanahan answered the call and became the latest Wings hero with two goals in Game 2. The second goal gave the Wings a 4-2 lead at 9:56 of the third period. Here is how it happened:

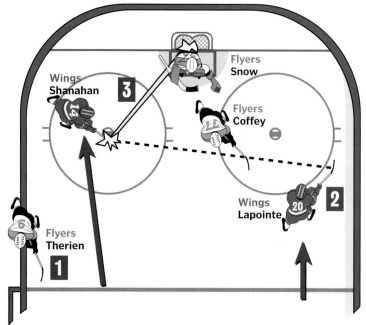

1 When defenseman Chris Therien (6) headed to the bench, the Wings caught the Flyers on a line change. Sergei Fedorov's quick pass from just inside the Wings' blue line got the play going.

2 Martin Lapointe (20) took Fedorov's pass at the red line and on the right wing, where he found himself on a two-on-one break with left wing Brendan Shanahan (14).

3 With only Paul Coffey (77) to beat, Lapointe, from the top of the right circle, fired a pass to Shanahan at the middle of the left circle. Shanahan one-timed a wrist shot past sprawling goalie Garth Snow (30).

adjust in the third period pretty well."

One of the Wings' best adjustments was something they have worked on throughout the playoffs. Even when the Flyers pressed, the Wings withstood the pressure because of tight checking and strong goaltending.

"I think we were able to remain composed throughout the game," Yzerman said. "Our goaltender made some real good saves. Our defensemen, I thought, were real solid in front of the net in blocking some shots and clearing pucks out. I don't think that

we controlled the game by any means, but we were able to remain relatively composed when the heat got on us."

The Wings return to Detroit with a chance to take a commanding series lead Thursday night. Although his team is in dire straits, Flyers captain Eric Lindros placed the pressure on the Wings.

"We haven't had a lead to work with yet," Lindros said. "But the pressure is on them with a 2-0 lead. They are supposed to win it. We'll go to Detroit and see what happens."

FORGOTTEN MEN LEAD 'UNNORMAL' WINGS TO FINALS

BY BOB WOJNOWSKI

The Detroit News

Larry Murphy wasn't supposed to be here. He was supposed to be on a golf course by now, the boos of Toronto fans rattling in his head.

Mike Vernon wasn't supposed to be here. He was supposed to be traded, or benched, or otherwise forgotten.

Joe Kocur wasn't supposed to be here. He was supposed to be in a rec league, relishing retirement.

Tomas Sandstrom wasn't supposed to be here.

He was supposed to be enjoying the off-season in Pittsburgh, contemplating his pending free agency.

Doug Brown wasn't supposed to be here. He was supposed to be too small, no longer in Scotty Bowman's plans, trade bait.

Aaron Ward wasn't supposed to be here. He was supposed to be on the bench, a rookie watching the playoffs.

But they're here, in the Stanley Cup Finals, and they're a big rea-

The Flyers' Paul Coffey (white helmet) and the Wings' Kirk Maltby (18) clash at the boards during the third period.

son the Red Wings are here. To win a Cup, it doesn't quite take a village, but it does take vigilance and persistence, and the Wings have at least half a dozen examples of it.

"When you get the opportunity, you try to make a difference," said Brown, who didn't play in 18 of the Wings' final 31 games, sat out the entire St. Louis series, then scored three goals against Anaheim. "We don't put the weight on one or two guys to carry us. It's important to persevere. Who knows where we'd be if guys went the other way?"

This is where Bowman's peculiar style pays dividends. Sure, he benches players without explanation,

annoys them, riles them. But he doesn't bury them. After Vernon played poorly (as did the rest of the Wings) in the Finals against New Jersey two years ago, then had a protracted contract squabble, many assumed he was gone. Bowman wanted him back for times such as these, when you need a veteran.

Sandstrom, acquired from Pittsburgh for Greg Johnson, has provided muscle and smarts. Ward, who didn't play much at midseason, has become a physical force on the blue line.

Murphy looked slow and soft when he arrived from Toronto at the trading deadline. But Bowman liked

his experience, and the defenseman has been dependable and occasionally dangerous. He had two assists in the Wings' 4-2 victory in Game 1.

"To get this far, it takes contributions from everyone," said Murphy, who won two Stanley Cups with Pittsburgh. "It's been that way throughout the history of the league."

Of course, you need help from all quarters. But these Wings are unique in their depth and versatility. They use four lines regularly and no one is dominating their scoring chart. Vernon has been excellent in goal, but the Wings aren't winning with one guy, or even a couple of guys, as teams generally do.

The last five Stanley Cup champions have been dominated by stars — Colorado (Joe Sakic, Patrick Roy), New Jersey (Claude Lemieux, Martin Brodeur), the Rangers (Mark Messier, Brian Leetch, Mike Richter), Montreal (Roy), Pittsburgh (Mario Lemieux).

For the Wings, the load has been spread from Sergei Fedorov to Slava Kozlov to Brendan Shanahan to Steve Yzerman to Igor Larionov to Vernon to ... Kocur.

Kocur, signed in December, scored on a breakaway in Game 1 and has been a physical presence throughout the playoffs. He was with the Rangers when they won in 1994 and he likes the look of this team.

"Teams that win do get those unnormal guys scoring," Kocur said. "It's an omen, or maybe it's just luck. You need luck. You need whatever it takes."

Whatever works. The Wings are dipping into all resources, tapping all sources. It might be unnormal, but it's working.

Yzerman, Shanahan help light the way

BY JOHN U. BACON

The Detroit News

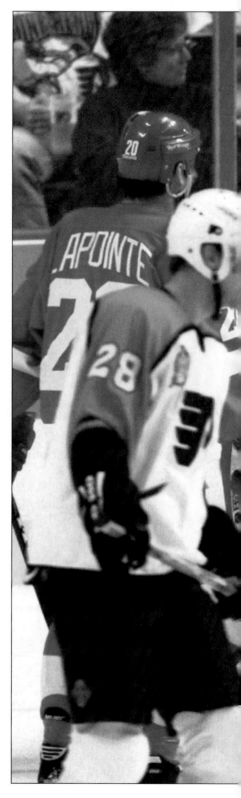

Probably no Red Wings had more pressure on them entering the playoffs than Steve Yzerman and Brendan Shanahan.

The Detroit fans and front office were waiting for Yzerman, the heart and soul of the Wings for almost a decade, to finally lead the team to a Stanley Cup. They expected Shanahan, the Wings' leading scorer, to be the long-missing piece to their playoff puzzle.

Through the first three series, Yzerman all but willed his team to victory in some games, but was virtually

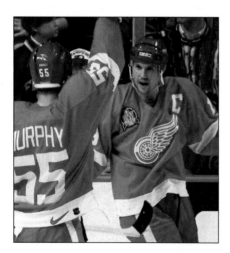

Defenseman Larry Murphy celebrates center Steve Yzerman's first-period power-play goal during the Wings' 4-2 victory.

invisible in others. Entering the Finals, his plus-minus rating stood at zero, and he hadn't had a point in five games.

Yzerman scored the final goal of the Red Wings' 4-2 victory in the first game of the Finals, then kept it going Tuesday night, beating Garth Snow on a scramble in front of the net. He also saved a goal in the second by tying up Rod Brind'Amour as a pass came through the slot.

After the game, Yzerman said the Wings' fruitless playoff runs the last two years have given them extra poise this time around. "We just feel a lot more comfortable," he said.

One reason is Shanahan, whom the Red Wings signed mainly to make them tougher in May and June. Shanahan did just that in the Wings' first 10 playoff games, getting four assists and three goals, two of them winners.

But before Tuesday night, Shanahan's points-per-game average had fallen steadily from 1.0 in the first series to .75 in the second to .67 in the third, against Colorado. Those aren't bad numbers, especially in the playoffs, but the trend wasn't promising with the most important games ahead.

Worse, in the five games preceding Game 2, Shanahan had two points: an assist in the 6-0 drubbing of Colorado in Game 4 and an open-net goal in Game 6.

So Shanahan's goal 1:37 into the first

period against Philadelphia on Tuesday provided a reassuring sign that he really was the clutch performer the Wings had hoped for when they traded for him.

Ironically, Shanahan's shot ricocheted off the foot of defenseman Paul Coffey, the trade bait the Wings used to get Shanahan. Coffey has been on the ice for six of the Wings' eight goals and in the penalty box for another.

Shanahan had a chance to put the Flyers away when he broke in alone on Snow in the second period. Snow dived at Shanahan, but Shanahan outwitted him by faking left and cutting right. Only a bouncing puck kept Shanahan from putting it away — and with it, possibly the game and the series.

"I guess I had about half a foot to shoot at, (but) I was trying to settle the puck down," Shanahan said.

The puck was nice and flat when Martin Lapointe fed Shanahan from the top of the right circle midway through the third period.

"Marty scored a lot of important goals from there, so the goalie has to challenge him," Shanahan said.

That explains why the net was so wide open for Shanahan when he redirected Lapointe's pass into it for the Wings' fourth goal.

After the game, Shanahan admitted he felt a lot of pressure since arriving in Detroit, but "it's better than not facing any pressure."

"Certainly it's a lot more fun when you're successful with it," he said.

Brendan Shanahan (14) is congratulated after scoring the Wings' first goal at 1:37 of the first period.

The Wings were in a mood to celebrate after Martin Lapointe's first-period goal.

ONE WIN AWAY

GAME 3	
Red Wings	**Flyers**
6	**1**
at Detroit	June 5, 1997

Victory puts Wings close to Stanley Cup

BY BOB WOJNOWSKI

The Detroit News

THIS ISN'T ABOUT PHILADELPHIA NOW, not that it ever was. The Flyers are still out there simply because the NHL requires an opponent, to make it official.

The Red Wings are skating alone now, chasing something only they and their fans can truly see and understand. This is how a 42-year wait ends, with a pursuit so dogged, so dominating, it hardly matters who's on the other side.

Three periods of formality Saturday night are all that stand between the Wings and a sweep to the Stanley Cup, a distance reduced to the slimmest margin because the Wings will not let up, not for one second or one shift. They belted the Flyers 6-1 Thursday night to seize a 3-0 lead in the Finals, and they did it as they've done it all playoffs, with a disciplined defense, with help from every area, led by the captain, who has scored in all three games.

Steve Yzerman bagged the first goal, Sergei Fedorov and Martin Lapointe had two apiece and by the end, the fans were feasting, famished by the wait. As the lead mounted, they cheered huge hits by Vladimir Konstantinov, an assist by Mike Vernon on the sixth goal and a circus shot by Brendan Shanahan, who scored from behind the net, flipping the puck off beleaguered goalie Ron Hextall.

Obviously, the Flyers have no one to stop the puck, no one to stop the relentless Red Tide. There are too many Wings with too much to prove and it starts with Yzerman, who has waited 14 years for that skate around the rink. It's close now, so close, the ever-intense captain almost flashed a smile.

"It's exciting, it's a lot of fun, but it's also nerve-wracking," said Yzerman, greeted by a prolonged ovation from fans longing to celebrate. "Things have gone pretty well but you can't afford to relax."

The Wings will get hockey's highest prize because they're loaded with players talented and poised, driven by all the emotions — revenge, redemption, respect.

Fedorov? It was said he was too laid-back, didn't care enough about

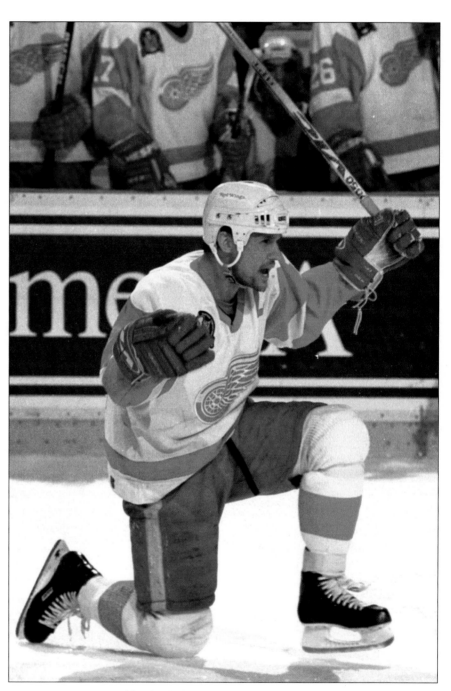

Steve Yzerman's goal ignited the Red Wings' outburst in Game 3.

the Cup. It was a rap ridiculously leveled on Russian players, and Fedorov, with three goals in the series and eight in the playoffs, has refuted plenty with perhaps the best all-around

hockey of his career.

Vernon? The general in net just will not blink at the huge Flyers. A fan held up a sign for the once-maligned goalie that read simply, "Vernon — I apologize." With the victory, Vernon all but clinched another year on his contract and sealed his standing in Wings lore.

Shanahan? He has scored big goals, has led with emotion and elbows, and in this series, he has matched Philly's overrated toughness.

Scotty Bowman? He came here four seasons ago, suffered three humbling losses in the playoffs, adapted and retooled his team and is poised to deliver the goods.

Of course, before Bowman and his players accept any praise, they do have that little formality.

"We're three-fourths of the way there, that's the way I look at it," Bowman said. "I told the players to enjoy the win for five minutes, then start thinking about the next game."

This was the danger game for the Wings because a Philadelphia victory could have turned the series. But the Wings and their fans aren't squandering any more time. As the Flyers were introduced before the game, the fans drowned out P.A. announcer Bud Lynch with chants of "Let's Go Red Wings!"

The Wings have no discernible nerves now and nothing to fear, not even Eric Lindros. The Big Red Machine is revved and the only thing that can slow it is overconfidence or a sudden spate of misfortune.

"We've been good all year at learning from past disappointments and turning them into positives," Darren McCarty said. "We were up 3-1 and lost to Colorado, so we're going to get ready for the game of our lives."

Really, this is about persistence and patience now, which seem like different qualities, but not for the Wings. They're patient enough to wait for their chances and their

GameThree: Where the Wings shot from

Period 1

● Goal ● Shot

Once again the Red Wings outshot their opponent, using puck movement and a stifling defense.

No.	Player	Shots
2	Slava Fetisov	1
5	Nicklas Lidstrom	3
14	Vyacheslav Kozlov	2
18	Brendan Shanahan	1
19	Vladimir Konstantinov	1
20	Doug Brown	1
25	Kirk Maltby	3
26	Steve Yzerman	3
28	Martin Lapointe	2
25	Darren McCarty	3
28	Tomas Sandstrom	2
33	Kris Draper	2
55	Larry Murphy	2
91	Sergei Fedorov	3

Period 2

Period 3

moment, persistent enough to create those chances, to demand that moment.

Even when Philadelphia grabbed a 1-0 lead, the Wings forced the play and didn't give the Flyers a chance to settle into a defensive shell. Not that it's possible to form a defensive shell when you've got a cracked shell in net. Hextall seems like a nice enough guy, but when he stops a puck these days, it's an accident.

You got the feeling early the only way the Wings could lose was if they gave it away. And in a shaky first period, they gave the Flyers four power plays, including a two-man advantage for 1:20. The Wings held firm, largely due to Yzerman's diligent penalty-killing, and when the Flyers failed, the wind and the will left them. The Wings — patiently,persistently — began to hammer.

It keeps coming back to the captain, exactly how it should be. He brought the franchise this far, he might as well push it the rest of the way. Two minutes after John LeClair provided the Flyers' first lead of the series, Yzerman took a quick pass from Vyacheslav Kozlov and fired it through the yawning gap between Hextall's legs.

Barely two minutes later, another Flyer giveaway led to another Detroit breakaway. We understand Philadelphia is the City of Brotherly Love, but really, the outpouring of compassion is startling. Karl Dykhuis lost the puck, Fedorov scooped it up and took a few strides before flipping a wrister past Hextall for a 2-1 lead.

Philly's weak two-man advantage followed and the Wings proceeded to take the game as if it was the clincher, swarming and smothering the Flyers. Lapointe, Mr. Feisty, grabbed the puck

Lapointe's big point

With the Red Wings ahead 2-1, Martin Lapointe hit the right post on a breakaway shortly after serving a tripping penalty at 18:43 of the first period. Lapointe then scored his first goal of the game with a shot between goalie Ron Hextall's legs, giving the Wings a 3-1 lead at 19:00 of the first period.

1 After Lapointe (20) hit the post, the Wings kept the puck in the Flyers' zone. Sergei Fedorov (91) got the puck near the right circle and pushed a pass ahead to Doug Brown (17).

2 Heading behind the net, Brown passed out front to Lapointe.

3 Standing in the slot between the Flyers' Mikael Renberg (19) and Chris Therien (6), Lapointe blasted a wrist shot past Hextall (27).

as he exited the penalty box and broke in alone. He fired it off the right post but — ah, persistence — immediately planted himself in front, awaited a beautiful pass from Doug Brown and beat Hextall to make it 3-1.

"We have to find a way to stop the bleeding, this is an embarrassment," said distraught Coach Terry Murray, who must know now that the Flyers are horribly flawed, and the Wings sense the kill. We have seen it so many times, with 13 victories in their

last 15 games. They're all about business, never let up, keep shooting until you see the dead in their eyes.

Shine the Cup and clear the mantle. After 42 years for the franchise, 14 years for the captain, the wait is down to three periods. We expect the Flyers to show up Saturday night, although we're not sure why.

They're merely the wait staff at the biggest party, four decades in the planning and the dreaming, three periods from popping the corks and the ghosts.

Martin Lapointe introduces the Flyers' Janne Niinimaa to the boards at Joe Louis Arena.

WINGS CAN TASTE CUP

BY CYNTHIA LAMBERT

The Detroit News

When Wings players went to sleep Thursday night, visions of hoisting the Stanley Cup likely were dancing in their heads.

On Saturday night at Joe Louis Arena, they can turn those dreams into reality, thanks to a 6-1 victory over the Philadelphia Flyers in Game 3 of the Stanley Cup Finals. The Wings lead the best-of-seven series three games to none.

"How can you not dream about it?" Darren McCarty said, his smile never fading. "You do that when you're a kid and you're going to do it now. We've put ourselves in a position to fulfill a lot of our dreams. But we also realize that's going to take a lot of hard work."

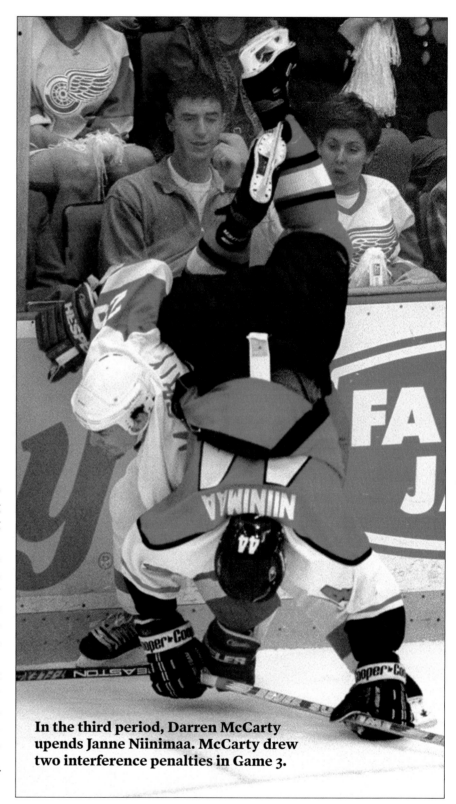

In the third period, Darren McCarty upends Janne Niinimaa. McCarty drew two interference penalties in Game 3.

Possibly just one more night of work if the Wings can complete a sweep of the Flyers on Saturday. Only once in the Finals has a team lost a series after taking a three-games-to-none lead. In 1942, the Wings took a 3-0 lead before Toronto rallied to win the series.

"We can't think we have four chances to win one game," forward Tomas Sandstrom said. "No team in the league is going to lay down and say, 'Go ahead. Take it.'"

In playoff hockey, the fourth victory is the toughest. Part of the reason is no team — even one as outplayed as the Flyers were Thursday night — will go through the motions. Also, visions of victory can sometimes hamper a team instead of inspire it.

"We've addressed it already, right after the game," assistant coach Mike Krushelnyski said. "Scotty (Bowman) said it and Stevie (Yzerman) said it. It's always toughest to get the final win. As a player, you have to block it out of your mind."

Yzerman said nervous feelings are hard to contain, but the team is focused on preventing them from taking over.

"I think our team has done a good job at getting prepared to play and remaining focused on playing and keeping our minds on hockey," Yzerman said. "We're enjoying ourselves, but again, it's a nerve-racking time."

Said Brendan Shanahan: "We're a team that's on a mission and it's not complete. You've got to battle (the thoughts) out of your mind."

Fighting that will be tougher than the front the Flyers put up Thursday night. Except for a power-play goal by John LeClair at 7:03 of the first period, the Flyers couldn't convert on their chances. The Wings gave them three

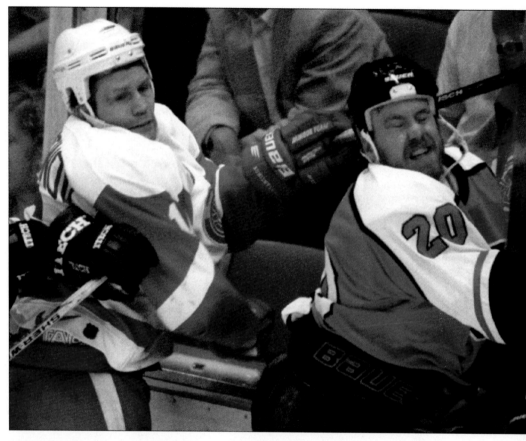

Wings defenseman Vladimir Konstantinov takes Flyers forward Trent Klatt into the glass.

more power plays in the first, and the Flyers had a two-man advantage for 1:20 after the Wings got goals from Steve Yzerman (power play) and Sergei Fedorov.

"In the first period, it seemed like a lot of bad things happened to us," Bowman said. "But we got some big goals."

Martin Lapointe scored his first of the game with a minute left in the first to give the Wings a 3-1 lead. As they had done earlier in the series, the Wings got an early goal in the second to squelch the Flyers' hopes of a comeback.

Fedorov got a power-play goal at 3:12 of the second, and Shanahan scored from one of his favorites spots — behind the net — at 19:12, banking the puck off Ron Hextall's knee to make it 5-1.

In the third, the Wings scored quickly — Lapointe again — to end the Flyers' night.

"We've got to find a way to stop the bleeding," Flyers Coach Terry Murray said. "The game was an embarrassment. We've got to give a better effort. The number of odd-man rushes against us was probably in double digits again. That's really unacceptable. We need to get our heads square and start thinking better. Right now, we all need some confidence. We really need to stick together as a team. We've been through hard times before, but you hate to see it in the Stanley Cup Finals."

Whether the Flyers, who look uninspired and defeated, can make a last stand remains to be seen. Whether the Wings can close the series at home Saturday night also is unknown.

But the Wings have been good at clinching in the playoffs this year. They ended series against St. Louis and Anaheim on their first try, and against Colorado on their second.

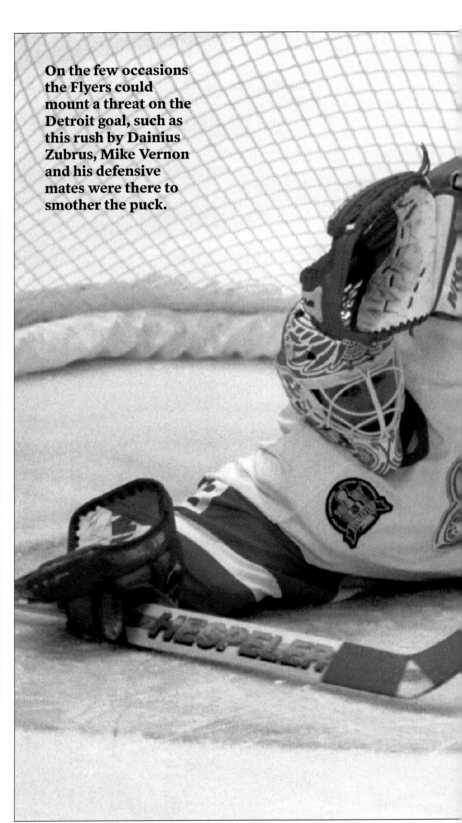

On the few occasions the Flyers could mount a threat on the Detroit goal, such as this rush by Dainius Zubrus, Mike Vernon and his defensive mates were there to smother the puck.

A Red Wings fan, who has dubbed himself Joe Spirit, pumps up the Joe Louis crowd while parading a homemade Stanley Cup through the stands.

FINALLY!

Wings sweep away Flyers — and demons — to become champions

BY BOB WOJNOWSKI

The Detroit News

AT THE END OF THE LONGEST WAIT, AFTER THE MAGICAL GOAL BY

GAME 4

Red Wings

2

Flyers

1

at Detroit
June 7, 1997

Darren McCarty and the splendid goaltending by Mike Vernon and the nightlong release of emotions raw and real, there was only one more thing to do, and only one person to do it.

After the longest wait, the longest skate. Captain Steve Yzerman finally hoisted the Stanley Cup on Saturday night, and as he skated, starting at center ice, slowly toward one goal, then to the other, he shook the silver trophy again and again, perhaps to make sure it was real. Around the rink he went, raising the Cup to every section, every fan, shaking loose theyears of disappointment, and the noise will ring forever.

Darren McCarty scored the winning goal at 13:02 of the second period.

Game Four: Where the Wings shot from

⚫ Goal   ⚫ Shot

The Red Wings outscored the Flyers by one in Game 4 and also outshot them by one, 28-27. Here is a breakdown of the Wings' shots.

No.	Player	Shots
2	Slava Fetisov	2
5	Nicklas Lidstrom	5
14	Brendan Shanahan	3
18	Kirk Maltby	1
19	Steve Yzerman	2
20	Martin Lapointe	1
25	Darren McCarty	2
26	Joe Kocur	2
28	Tomas Sandstrom	1
33	Kris Draper	1
55	Larry Murphy	2
91	Sergei Fedorov	6

Period 1

Period 2

Period 3

This was a 41-year drought that had become the singular obsession of a city, a team and a man. The wait is over, the weight is lifted, the nightmares end.

"Sometimes you hold your dreams way out there and you wonder if it can ever be as good as you dream," Yzerman said. "It was almost like I wanted to sit back and watch it all and not miss a minute of it."

And those repeated shakes of the Cup?

Yzerman smiled.

"The thing was getting heavy. My arms were giving out."

They were the only parts that ever gave out, as Yzerman's passion sparked a franchise and took it where it hadn't been since 1955. The captain had a cause, and this morning, the Red Wings have the Cup, and sometime around mid-July, the Philadelphia Flyers might recognize what hit them. Spurred by emotion and talent and the relentless red tide of history, the Wings skated through all barriers and took the trophy they had to have.

They won it the only way they could, with contributions from every man on the roster, with Vernon stopping every Philadelphia foray, with all four lines and every defensemen making plays when they had to be made. There was Nicklas Lidstrom, the quiet blue-liner, breaking the tension and the scoreless tie late in the first period with a vicious slap shot. There was McCarty, perhaps the team's most underrated player, grabbing the puck and faking defenseman Janne Niinimaa and then faking goalie Ron Hextall and then sprawling to the ice as he scored.

That was the prettiest snapshot from the Wings' 2-1 victory that offi-

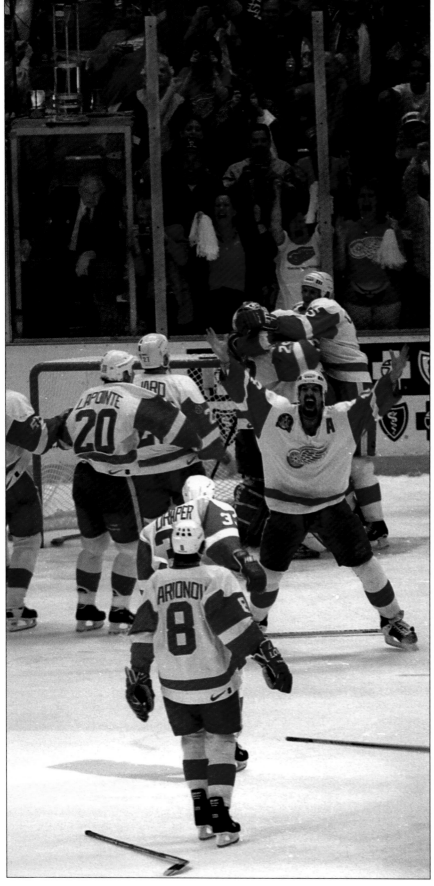

Let the celebration begin: Brendan Shanahan was up in arms after the Wings ended their Stanley Cup drought.

cially broomed the Flyers, and it was framed by players so determined and dominant, it was scary. Vernon, the playoff MVP, was the man who made the important plays on this night, stopping 26 shots and capping a phenomenal playoff run. Scotty Bowman was the general behind the bench, making history by winning his seventh Cup with his third franchise, something no one has ever done.

When it was over, the 63-year-old legend donned skates and took a spin with the Cup himself, something else he had never done.

"I always wanted to be an NHL player and skate with the Cup, and you never know how many chances you'll get," he said. "So I figured I'd go for it. It was pretty heavy, but light, too."

If Bowman was the man with the whip, the captain was the guy who kept it all together, who stood up and spoke when necessary, who was always there, through the lean years and mean years, when he was the only commodity this franchise had.

Now, Yzerman is surrounded by the finest collection of hockey players in the world, and although his scoring role has diminished, his impact never did. It's funny, when he finally gets to smile the broadest, he's missing a tooth, the second dislodging of his career. He gave sweat and blood and teeth and this is why he stayed all these years, 14 in all, through disappointment after disappointment, injury after injury, trade rumor after trade rumor, to take that skate.

He needed a prodding from Brendan Shanahan to begin the longest skate, and when he was done, he handed the Cup to Slava Fetisov and Igor Larionov, the two Russian legends.

"I kind of wanted to do it as a team," Yzerman said, "but it was kind of neat to do it alone."

These Wings did nothing alone, but the "Ste-vie! Ste-vie!" chants will ring the longest, and finally, the cheering wasn't a sentimental gesture for hard work in troubled times, but appreciation for taking a championship team the final step.

Yzerman is the symbol, the lasting image, but he's not a singular star, and that's what makes these Wings unique. They have so many viable components, from the power-skating Sergei Fedorov, to the playmaking Larionov, to the powerful Shanahan, to big-bodied bangers such as McCarty, Martin Lapointe, Kirk Maltby and Joey Kocur. They have punch along the blue line with Nicklas Lidstrom and Vladimir Konstantinov and savvy veterans in Larry Murphy and Fetisov.

This is a team with so many factions on the ice, few off it. And make no mistake. It was bonded by that March 26 game against Colorado, when McCarty did what he had to do, pounding the life out of Claude Lemieux, pounding it into the Wings.

The Wings had a cause, just like the captain. They erased the stink of their playoff humblings and convinced themselves something special was possible. Now, no more questions, no more sad explanations. No more reminiscing about the good ol' days when the Wings won all those championships back in the '50s. The good ol' days are now, resurrected by a team that could not, would not be denied.

Grab a broom and sweep out the old nightmares. Stanley finally came home, delivered by a captain with a cause, and a team that finally found its way.

Hot goaltending has crowd chanting 'Vernie'

Stanley Cup MVPs

Year	Name	Team
1965	Jean Beliveau	Montreal
1966	*Roger Crozier	Red Wings
1967	Dave Keon	Toronto
1968	*Glenn Hall	St. Louis
1969	Serge Savard	Montreal
1970	Bobby Orr	Boston
1971	Ken Dryden	Montreal
1972	Bobby Orr	Boston
1973	Yvan Cournoyer	Montreal
1974	Bernie Parent	Philadelphia
1975	Bernie Parent	Philadelphia
1976	*Reggie Leach	Philadelphia
1977	Guy Lafleur	Montreal
1978	Larry Robinson	Montreal
1979	Bob Gainey	Montreal
1980	Bryan Trottier	New York
1981	Butch Goring	New York
1982	Mike Bossy	New York
1983	Bill Smith	New York
1984	Mark Messier	Edmonton
1985	Wayne Gretzky	Edmonton
1986	Patrick Roy	Montreal
1987	*Ron Hextall	Philadelphia
1988	Wayne Gretzky	Edmonton
1989	Al MacInnis	Calgary
1990	Bill Ranford	Edmonton
1991	Mario Lemieux	Pittsburgh
1992	Mario Lemieux	Pittsburgh
1993	Patrick Roy	Montreal
1994	Brian Leetch	NY Rangers
1995	Claude Lemieux	New Jersey
1996	Joe Sakic	Colorado
1997	**Mike Vernon**	Red Wings

* Played on losing team in the finals.

By JERRY GREEN

The Detroit News

As Mike Vernon flipped and stopped another puck with his body on the ice, a guy in the lower bowl at Joe Louis Arena waved the sign of the season:

"VERNON I APOLOGIZE."

Of course, the sign had another message written on the opposite side — sort of a two-faced sign.

The same hockey connoisseurs who have been chanting "Vernie, Vernie, Vernie" these past few weeks in the Red Wings' stampede to the Stanley Cup are the same who condemned Vernon two years ago.

Vernon was brilliant again as the Red Wings clinched the Cup for the first time in 42 years with Saturday night's 2-1 victory in a sweep of the Flyers.

"I saw the sign, and I kind of chuckled," Vernon said after he received the Conn Smythe Trophy as the most valuable player in the playoffs. "It was in the back of the minds of all of us, two years ago and how devastating it was to lose to Jersey.

"I don't know who the guy was, but I accept the apology."

Early on, he kept the Red Wings in the game, foiling shot after shot as Philadelphia had a 6-1 advantage in shots. It was the

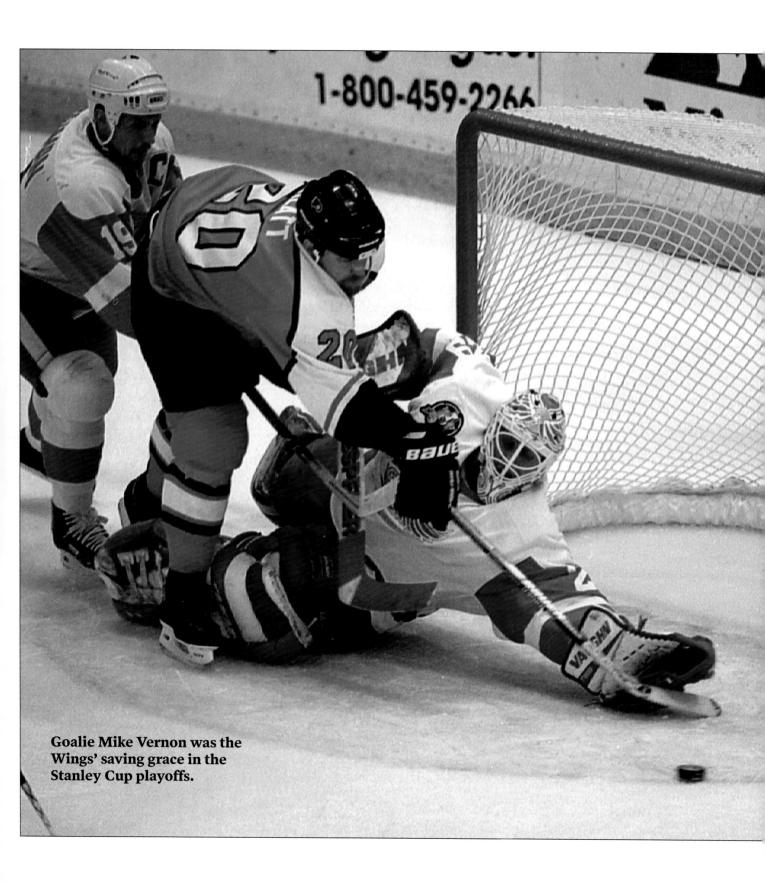

1-800-459-2266

Goalie Mike Vernon was the Wings' saving grace in the Stanley Cup playoffs.

Flyers' heaviest pressure of the series. In one sequence the Flyers surrounded him. The puck went high and Vernon outreached the brawnier Flyers to grab the puck.

And then he thwarted clear shots by Mikael Renberg, Janne Niinimaa and Colin Forbes as the Flyers sought to overhaul the Wings and salvage the game. The Flyers couldn't score until the last 14.8 seconds of the game, with electricity crackling in the building, when Eric Lindros finally got his only goal of the series.

Vernon boosted his playoff record to 16-4, three victories more than he had in the regular season.

Some difference from two years ago in the Finals, the devastation Vernon couldn't forget.

Back then the complaint was a porous 5-hole. The critics recognized that the sweeping Devils blasted too many radar-controlled pucks between Vernon's pads.

Then again, they are the same faithful who welcomed him when he joined the Red Wings via trade from the Calgary Flames in 1994. That was shortly after they chased Tim Chevaldae out of town with their constant jeers.

The key to winning in the playoffs, to winning the Cup itself, is hot goaltending. Hockey ancients swear that is true, citing hot goaltenders of yesteryear such as Terry Sawchuk, Jacques Plante, Gump Worsley, Ken Dryden and, yes, Patrick Roy.

Vernon got hot at the right time.

"Yeah, it is a big challenge for Mike," Red Wings' Coach Scotty Bowman had said to the media.

"... he had a big challenge when he came into Detroit and our goaltending at the time was maligned quite a bit. Some justified and some unjustified ... He bounces back pretty well."

Bounces back indeed.

After all, Bowman, with his habit of tinkering with his goalies, snubbed Vernon through most of the regular season. But Bowman has a sense of hockey history with its hot-goalie theory. In February, Bowman started priming the Red Wings for the playoffs. He started playing Vernon in preference over Chris Osgood. How many nights had the fans chanted: "Ozzie, Ozzie, Ozzie," as Vernon sat dressed in his hockey armor, ignored on the bench?

Vernon was on the brink of becoming the 13th goaltender in NHL history to win 300 games. It was an elusive milestone. In March, he hyperextended a knee in a loss to Anaheim. He missed four games. When he returned in Chicago on March 23, the Blackhawks fired four shots at him. Three went in. Bowman yanked him 7:19 into the first period.

Then came the bloody night of March 26 against Colorado. When the brawling started, Vernon sped out and nailed Roy. He gave away 27 pounds and three inches to Roy. When the fight ended, it was Roy who bled.

It was a simple matter of guts.

And when the game ended in overtime, Vernon had his 300th victory at last. In tribute, Roy, his rival for nearly a dozen years, dispatched the winning puck down ice to Vernon, a souvenir.

McCARTY'S GOAL IS GAME 4 HIGHLIGHT

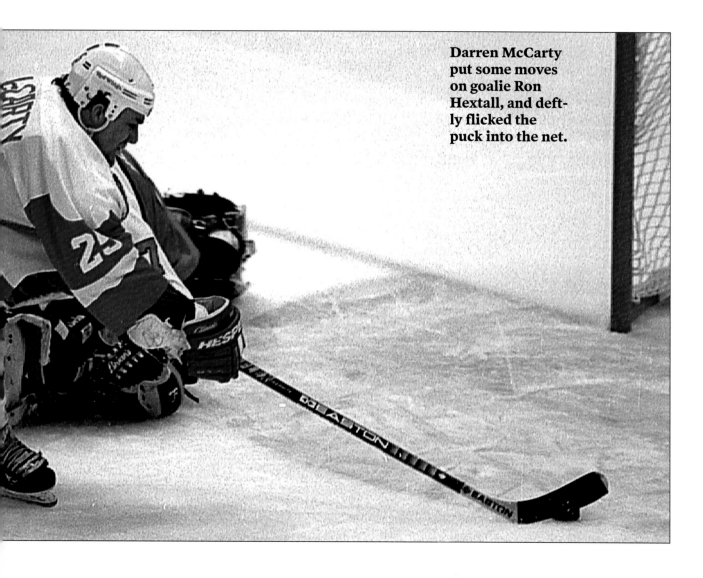

Darren McCarty put some moves on goalie Ron Hextall, and deftly flicked the puck into the net.

BY DAVE DYE

The Detroit News

When Darren McCarty scores a goal like he did Saturday night, you know it's time to start engraving the names on the Stanley Cup.

McCarty's third goal in 20 playoff games gave the Red Wings a two-goal lead on the way to a Cup-clinching 2-1 victory over the Philadelphia Flyers.

This was not the typical goal that McCarty scores, at least not since he was a peewee. It was the kind that Steve Yzerman or Sergei Fedorov scores. Or Wayne Gretzky or Mario Lemieux.

Who knew Darren McCarty had moves like that?

Certainly not Flyers defenseman Janne Niinimaa, who was so embarrassed and frustrated that he whacked his stick on the crossbar.

McCarty skated up on a rush, used a deke move and went to his left to get around Niinimaa, who fell to the ice. Then he carried the puck back to his right side and around goalie Ron Hextall.

"Every blind squirrel finds a nut," McCarty said while spraying champagne during the dressing-room celebration.

"It's happy, happy job," he said as he hugged teammate Joe Kocur. "Indescribable. Show me the money. Show me the Cup.

"No more '55. Now it's '97. This is what it's all about. We've worked hard all year. It's a great bunch of guys.

"This isn't just for us. It's for the city of Detroit, all our fans who stuck behind us."

The Wings scored many soft goals against the Flyers in the Finals. But McCarty's belongs on the highlight reel for the ages.

"I think he had to dream that one up," Kocur said.

Said Kirk Maltby: "That goal was definitely the turning point for this game."

McCarty, the Wings' second pick (46th overall) in the 1992 draft, first came up to the NHL because of his ability to be an enforcer-type player and fight. But he's shown he can be productive in other ways, too, which is why he took on a larger role this season after the Wings traded other forwards such as Dino Ciccarelli.

McCarty, 25, had a career-best 49 points in the regular season. He had six points in the playoffs this year, and has 21 in his career (11 goals). He scored the winning goal in a pivotal 5-2 victory in Game 5 of the first round against St. Louis.

McCarty also scored the biggest goal of the regular season, when he beat Patrick Roy in overtime for a 6-5 victory in the memorable March 26 game against Colorado.

In that game, he also beat up Claude Lemieux as payback for his hit on Draper in last season's playoff. That night is considered a turning point for the Wings' season.

"Max has been doing this for us all year long," Draper said. "He scored huge goals for us in the playoffs and now, obviously, tonight is icing on the cake.

"It is good to see a guy like that get a big goal in a big game. Everyone loves him in the dressing room. You can tell by the reaction when he scored."

McCarty could barely wait for Saturday night to get there. After Thursday's Game 3 victory, he said it would be a dream come true.

"I'd like to play right now," McCarty said as he was bouncing up and down.

Saturday morning, about nine hours before game time, McCarty said, "If you can't get up for this game, you might as well be six feet under."

"This has been great for the whole community," McCarty said of the interest in the Wings. "It's a great thing. It's bringing a lot of people together. Instead of giving people the finger when they cut you off on the highway, people are now saying, 'OK, you go ahead.' It's a great thing to see."

When the clock struck zero Saturday night on the Joe Louis Arena scoreboard, about 10:50 p.m, McCarty threw off his gloves. He grabbed his helmet and flipped it in the air. Then he raced for the wild celebration at the Wings' net.

It was no longer a dream. It was a Stanley Cup championship for Darren McCarty, the man with more moves than anyone had ever seen before.

McCarty seals it

With smooth moves, Darren McCarty gave the Wings a 2-0 lead in their Stanley Cup-clinching win. Here's how he did it:

1 Before taking a big hit from the Flyers' Eric Lindros (88), Tomas Sandstrom (28) found Darren McCarty (25) open in the neutral zone. His pass hit McCarty just before McCarty hit center ice.

2 As he gained the Flyers' zone, McCarty was met by Flyers defenseman Janne Niinimaa (44), with defenseman Michel Petit (8) trailing on the play.

3 McCarty faked out Niinimaa by going to his left, then back to his right. Flyers goalie Ron Hextall (27) tried to halt McCarty by moving to his right, but McCarty pulled the puck back and went to Hextall's left and scored with a wrist shot at 13:02 of the second period.

WINGS TAKE FLIGHT IN CUP FINALE

Wings captain Steve Yzerman hoists the Stanley Cup toward team owners Mike and Marian Ilitch.

BY CYNTHIA LAMBERT

The Detroit News

The Red Wings will no longer use memories of failing in the playoffs as their motivation.

Now they have the real thing — success and the Stanley Cup.

In convincing fashion, the Wings claimed their first Stanley Cup since 1955 with a 2-1 victory over the Philadelphia Flyers on Saturday night at Joe Louis Arena, sweeping them out of town in four games.

The prestigious trophy was presented by NHL Commissioner Gary Bettman to captain Steve Yzerman, who hoisted it over his head for everyone to see. After

spending 14 years as the leader and inspiration of this team, Yzerman finally could discard all the failures and hold high hockey's most prized possession.

"I don't know how to describe how I feel," Yzerman said. "I'm glad the game is over, but I wish it never ended."

Yzerman shared the trophy and the accomplishment with his teammates, particularly goaltender Mike Vernon, who appeared in every playoff game this year, going 16-4.

Vernon also was rewarded with the Conn Smythe Trophy, presented to the playoff MVP. He had a 1.79 goals-against average in the playoffs and a .944 save percentage in the Finals.

Throughout this postseason, the

Wings had talked of how losing to New Jersey in the 1995 Finals, when they were swept, and the Western Conference finals to Colorado last season was their motivation. And as each opponent — St. Louis, Anaheim and then Colorado — was dispatched in this postseason, the Wings gained momentum. By the time they faced the Flyers, their game was honed.

"The experience of the last two years was huge," Wings Coach Scotty Bowman said. "The team was more prepared."

Bowman, who won his seventh Cup with an NHL-record third team, said he has not decided whether he will return next season as head coach. He said he would like to leave the game the way his idol, Toe Blake, did. Blake, who won eight Cups with Montreal, retired after leading the Canadiens to the 1968 title.

As they did in each of the previous three games of the series, the Wings scored on a long shot. On Saturday night, Nicklas Lidstrom beat Ron Hextall with a shot from the blue line at 19:27 of the first period. Darren McCarty made it 2-0 at 13:02 of the second period on a fabulous rush. He made enough moves to leave the Flyers' defense helpless and Hextall far out of the net.

With 14.8 seconds left, Eric Lindros scored for the Flyers, who had pulled Hextall with 1:48 left for an extra attacker.

The Wings led 1-0 after the first period on Lidstrom's goal. They started strongly in the second, initiating the play instead of reacting. But the score remained tight.

That is, until The Rush.

With the puck at the boards in the Wings' zone, Tomas Sandstrom withstood a hit to make a perfect pass to McCarty beyond the blue line. McCarty sped through the neutral zone and into the Flyers' end. Defenseman Janne Niinimaa stood between McCarty and Hextall, but McCarty took care of that with a quick move to the left that sent Niinimaa spinning to the ice.

McCarty drew Hextall out to the left, pulled the puck to his forehand and cut right. McCarty's move was so quick that Hextall was still out of the crease when the shot went into an open net at 13:02.

What was McCarty thinking about during his rush?

"I don't know," he said. "I think I moved to the right and lost the puck, so then I headed left. Before I knew it, I was right on Hextall.

"Don't expect that all the time."

Sergei Fedorov, right, led the Wings with six points in the Finals.

FEDOROV'S TOUGH SEASON ENDS WITH A FLOURISH

BY JOHN NIYO

The Detroit News

He already had the fancy skates. He already had the fancy commercials. He already had the fancy car.

Soon now, Sergei Fedorov will have the fancy ring, too. Diamonds are forever, eh, Sergei?

His smile Saturday night said it all, embellishing his statistics — three goals and three assists in the Finals, eight goals and 12 assists overall.

Not a bad way to finish what has been, in Fedorov's words, his "most difficult season."

Fedorov, 27, is in the final year of his contract. And, fresh off last year's playoff disappointment, he and his agent, Mike Barnett, spent the better part of the early months this season haggling over Fedorov's worth with the Red Wings organization.

There were brief glimpses of this former Hart Trophy winner — most notably that five-goal performance

Dec. 26 against Washington, when he scored all the Wings' goals in a 5-4 overtime victory.

But more often, Fedorov was a portrait of unhappiness, struggling to find his scoring touch, banished to Scotty Bowman's checking line and quietly fuming at the insult.

At one point, he remarked that the third-line status was "an honor," although everyone within earshot could detect the sarcasm.

Then came Bowman's experiment late in the season, when he switched Fedorov to defense, even starting the playoffs with this Nike poster boy on the blue line.

Again, Fedorov kept quiet, or at least relatively so. He said he was happy getting more minutes — as many as 30 a game — and shrugged off questions about his winter of discontent.

"I mean, he's a different person," said teammate Darren McCarty, whose locker is next to Fedorov's in the dressing room. "That's what some people don't understand. He's not like everybody else.

"Compared to me, I'm more outgoing, more emotional, a scream-and-yell guy. Sergei is more to himself. People can't read him."

Fedorov scored the two most important goals in Game 3 of the Finals — unassisted on the winner in the first period, and with a nifty move for the Wings' fourth goal to seal it.

"You got to give the guy a break," McCarty said Saturday morning. "He can be the best player in the league when he wants to. He seizes his opportunities. Last game (Game 3 against Philadelphia), he proved it. It was the biggest game of our career, and he rose to the occasion."

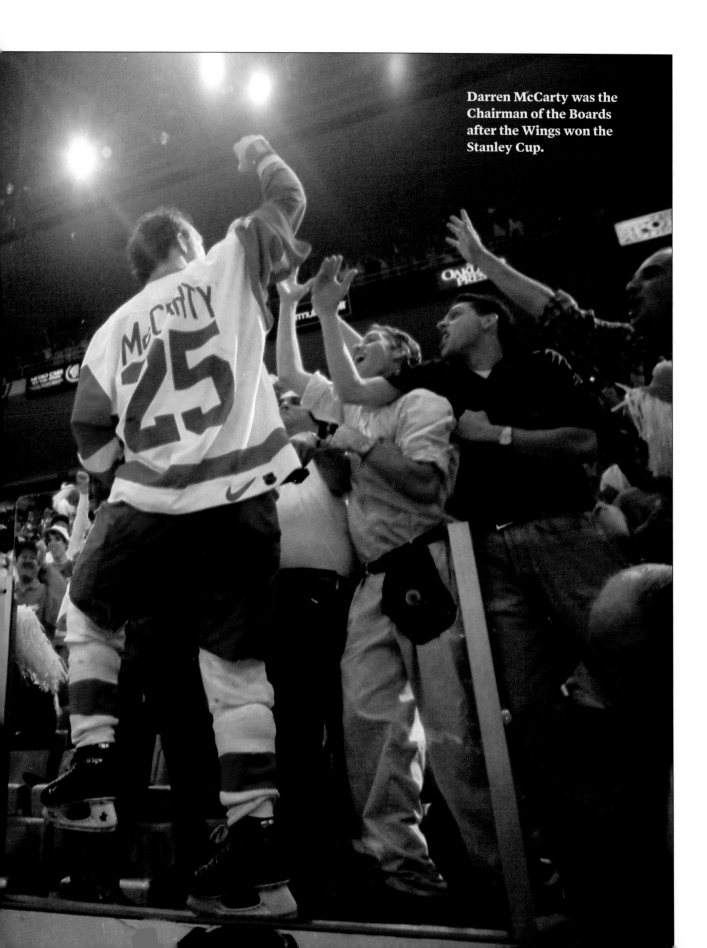

Darren McCarty was the Chairman of the Boards after the Wings won the Stanley Cup.

Stevie Y.

Quiet captain speaks volumes in leading the Wings to the Cup

BY JERRY GREEN

The Detroit News

And then it happened. The guardians, wearing white gloves, opened the strong box that protected the 104-year-old Stanley Cup. The trophy was set, gleaming in the bright lights, onto the table at center ice. And Steve Yzerman, the Captain, skated over to receive it.

At last, long last.

The confetti floated from the rafters. The Red Wings were Stanley Cup champions, for the first time since 1955, 10 years before Yzerman was born. They had swept the Philadelphia Flyers in four games, with sheer ice control, poise, discipline.

Yzerman hesitated with the Cup, uncertain. And then he raised it toward his teammates and the cheering multitudes. He caressed it and put it above his head again, pumped it upward in triumph. And then he skated around the ice at Joe Louis Arena in the captain's championship lap.

It was a ritual he knew well. He had watched, in envy, for years as Wayne Gretzky and Mario Lemieux and Mark Messier and Joe Sakic, captains of other conquering teams, had taken the Cup on its annual tour around the rink.

"As long as I could remember, since I was 5 years old, I watched the Stanley Cup, I've stayed up, made a point of watching it presented, watched the celebration in the locker room, and always dreamed that maybe I'd get there," Yzerman said.

"But ... and sometimes you wonder if you'll ever get there. So I guess, as the game was going on, and when we finally won, it's almost like I wanted to sit back and watch the whole thing and not miss a minute of it, and not forget any of it. I don't know if it can ever be as good as the dream, but I'd rather sit back and just watch everybody. I don't want to miss any of it."

Steve Yzerman is a quiet captain. He keeps his emotions harnessed. He seldom shows jubilation, except when he lifts his hockey stick and smiles after scoring a goal. He joined the Red Wings when he was 18. At 21, was captain of the team. He has suffered the indignity of trade rumors, injury, defeat.

And now, at the end of his 14th sea-

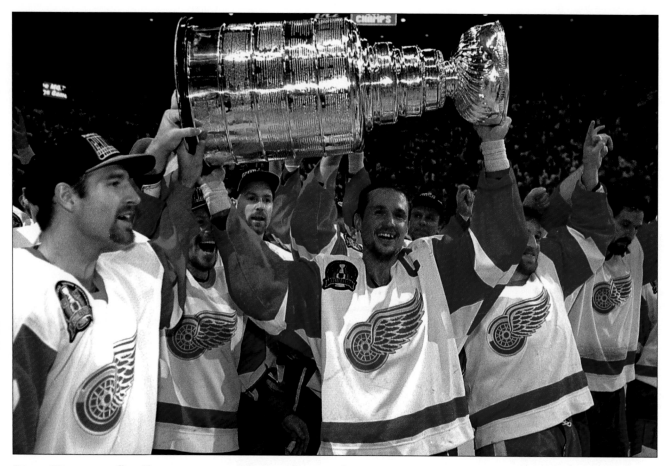

Steve Yzerman finally gets to experience the Stanley Cup presentation he had always watched on television.

son, he had his grip on the Stanley Cup. At last. He began his solo skate, slowly, searching into the grandstands, into the multitudes.

"I was looking for my parents," he said. "And then I was looking for my wife in the corner."

He toured to the far side of the rink, to the roar of the crowd, as his team waited for him to return.

"The thing was getting heavy," Yzerman said. "My arms were giving out."

He skated around and handed the Cup to Slava Fetisov, one of the Red Wings' celebrated and sometimes maligned, Russian Five. Fetisov is

pushing 40, a defenseman whose craggy face displayed a series of stick scars from more than 20 years of high-level hockey wars. He had won Olympic and world championships for the Soviet Union. He played for the renowned Red Army team, or CSKA, in Moscow. Then with bitterness, he broke with the Red Army team and led the stream of Russian hockey defectors to North America — just as communism collapsed and the Soviet Union fragmented.

It was to Fetisov that Captain Yzerman handed the trophy to begin the tradition in which every player has his turn to hoist, kiss and cherish

the Cup. Fetisov placed one side of the Cup into the hands of Igor Larionov, his 36-year-old teammate with the Red Army and the Red Wings. They skated in tandem with the Cup.

Through the years of the Red Wings' failures to win, critics had faulted the Russians for not comprehending the spirit of the Stanley Cup.

"As far as giving it to Slava," said Yzerman, "the last couple of days — you try not to think about anything but the game, you've got a million things running through your mind, and I got caught up with who should I hand the Cup off to?"

Always a potent shot, Yzerman had to change his game under Coach Scotty Bowman. Without complaint and despite the critics, he traded points for victories.

"I thought of a few different players. Slava jumped to my mind because of what he's done. He and Igor, what kind of guys they are. I really respect them, what they've done and how they've handled themselves, and they set an example in their work ethic and their attitude for the young Russian players. And they've been real leaders on our team.

"I don't know if Slava's coming back next year or not. But after the great career he's had I wanted him to get the trophy. He's done everything in the world of hockey, and this is the most important thing, so I wanted to give it to him."

The symbolism was captured. Steve Yzerman, through the years, had been a captain criticized often for not being loud or sufficiently vocal in his leadership. He explained so often that he stresses leadership by example.

Part of his quiet front is shyness. Part of it is modesty. He was born in British Columbia, grew up in Nepean, Ontario, in suburban Ottawa. He was raised well in citizenship. He was raised well in hockey.

Seldom has he rebuked his teammates. But he did in the first round of the 1997 playoffs, when they were deadlocked after a 4-0 loss to St. Louis. He stood up and challenged his team, urging them to start producing. He included himself in the criticism.

Seldom has he jabbed at a player. But in the 1997 series with Colorado, Sergei Fedorov rode into the boards, damaging his ribs. Fedorov could barely breath. He was assisted to the dressing room. He was considered done for the game. Yzerman approached him after the first period: "Sergei, we need you." Fedorov soon returned. He was brilliant when he got back. He scored the winning goal

Yzerman challenged and prodded his teammates during the playoffs. His speech after a loss to St. Louis in the opening series sparked the Wings.

that eliminated the Avalanche.

Seldom has he engaged in hockey's rough stuff, the fighting. But one night, years ago when a brawl broke out, Yzerman was seen punching the Canadiens' Bobby Smith in a corner of the Forum.

It is leadership.

And as Yzerman led, each of the Red Wings did his bit with the Stanley Cup. Even Scotty Bowman, with his seventh Stanley Cup championship as a coach, put on his skates to ride with the trophy. Then the Cup was taken from the ice. It was transported into the Red Wings dressing room, into the back, where on the stationary bikes Yzerman had pedaled for hours, days, restrengthening muscle from his various injuries.

The bandwagon rolled into the champions' dressing room soon after the Cup. Folks who had recently discovered that water freezes at 32

degrees Fahrenheit to form ice poured into the room. It was jammed, sweltering from the TV lights, champagne spraying around the room, drenching the red shirts and dresses of the interlopers.

Yzerman stood out front among the crowd. His face was soaked with sweat. He had the very beginnings of another playoff goatee on his chin and cheeks. He had stripped off his No. 19 jersey with the captain's C on the left front shoulder. He wore a cap that read: "Stanley Cup CHAMPS." And he patiently endeavored to deliver the feelings of his past frustrations to the media marvels who were about to reach him. Mostly, he expressed relief — that it was his turn and he was relishing it.

"I love this team," he said.

"I was going to feel all this different stuff. It happened too quick. When I started playing as a kid, I dreamed of

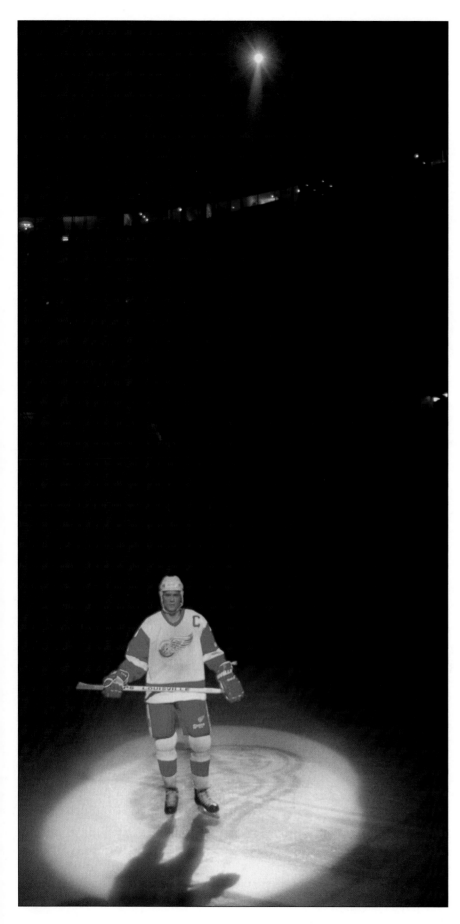

Yzerman, 32, has been in the spotlight with the Red Wings for 14 seasons. He was named captain of the team at the age of 21.

the NHL and the Stanley Cup. But it was filled with a lot of disappointments ... a lot of tough losses. I think I'm a better player for it.

"The hardest part is sitting around waiting. I can usually sleep the afternoon before a game. I couldn't today. I just wanted to be left alone. Let's get on the ice and play.

"We've had some disappointments and we've broken people's hearts. People would always say, as good as you are, you didn't win the Cup.

"Now people can't say that."

Yzerman spoke as the bedlam went on around him. It was after midnight, early Sunday morning. Brendan Shanahan came up and spoke words into Yzerman's ear. Shanahan was still dressed in full game regalia, his No. 14 jersey, his ice skates.

A half dozen mini tape recorders nearly brushed Yzerman's whiskers. Some reporters stood in the second circle around him, scratching his words into their notebooks. Fans pushed in.

They, the hockey fans, are passionate people. In Detroit, they are vigorously devoted to their team. They are fickle, of course. In the few years past they had rabidly cheered the Red Wings when they had hugely successful regular seasons, then were defeated in the playoffs. They felt disgraced when the Red Wings went out in the first round to the ancient-rival Maple Leafs one year, then the upstart San Jose Sharks the next. They bled and cursed when the Red Wings reached the Stanley Cup

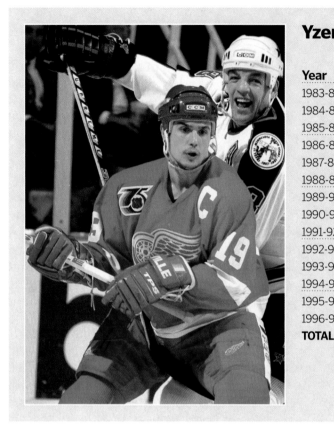

Yzerman's career numbers

Year	Team	Regular Season					Playoffs				
		GP	G	A	P	PM	GP	G	A	P	PM
1983-84	Detroit	80	39	48	87	33	4	3	3	6	0
1984-85	Detroit	80	30	59	89	58	3	2	1	3	2
1985-86	Detroit	51	14	28	42	16	-	-	-	-	-
1986-87	Detroit	80	31	59	90	43	16	5	13	18	8
1987-88	Detroit	64	50	52	102	44	3	1	3	4	6
1988-89	Detroit	80	65	90	155	61	6	5	5	10	2
1989-90	Detroit	79	62	65	127	79	-	-	-	-	-
1990-91	Detroit	80	51	57	108	34	7	3	3	6	4
1991-92	Detroit	79	45	58	103	64	11	3	5	8	12
1992-93	Detroit	84	58	79	137	44	7	4	3	7	4
1993-94	Detroit	58	24	58	82	36	3	1	3	4	0
1994-95	Detroit	47	12	26	38	40	15	4	8	12	0
1995-96	Detroit	80	36	59	95	64	18	8	12	20	4
1996-97	Detroit	81	22	63	85	78	20	7	6	13	4
TOTAL		**1,023**	**539**	**801**	**1,340**	**694**	**113**	**46**	**65**	**111**	**46**

Finals for the first time in 29 years in 1995, then were swept in four games by the New Jersey Devils. And they vilified their team when the Red Wings were defeated in 1996 in the bitter Western Conference final series by the hated Colorado Avalanche.

Yzerman was among those condemned by anonymous fans, callers to sports talk shows: "He never turns up for the playoffs." "He's always hurt."

Uncontrolled rumors abounded that the Red Wings would trade him.

"The last five years, you didn't want to be recognized," Yzerman said to his audience. "I put a hat on, glasses on. You don't want people to recognize you.

"A couple of years ago I went to Las Vegas after the playoffs. I don't remember which year. I was at the craps table. Two old guys from Windsor came by and saw me. They said, 'You don't want to play at this table. There's no luck at this table.' "

About that time, Yzerman sat with a single reporter in a rare interview, speaking his inner feelings.

"Yeah, always," he said about watching the Stanley Cup presentation ceremony on television in his home in suburban Detroit each spring. "You're driving down the road and some song comes on the radio and you're thinking about it. I've always thought about that, every year.

"Every year I've always tried, no matter what I'm doing, no matter what I've seen or missed of the playoffs, I always try to make a point of seeing the final game — or the end of the final game — because I enjoy see-

ing the Stanley Cup presented.

"I enjoy seeing the Super Bowl, or the world championship in baseball or basketball.

"I like seeing the finish part. Yeah, I think everybody, whatever they dream of, always pictures it the same way.

"I've got friends who've won the Cup, and it's interesting to see people when they win and how they react. To see them in the summer and ask what it was like. Just to see what it's like ...

"Very envious ...

"I found that the last couple of years, as the hype and expectation for our team has grown, there are setbacks along the way. And although they seem the end of the world at the time, you survive, improve and improve, and at some point, you get to reach your goal.

"But every year, as we've kind of faded in the playoffs, it grows a little more imperative — I guess in my mind — to accomplish what you want to accomplish."

Now, after 14 years, mature at 32, he had accomplished what he wanted to accomplish. He did it as a player who had been required to adjust his style, make alternate use of his skills.

Through his first 10 seasons in Detroit, Yzerman's primary function was to score goals. He became one of the more prolific scorers in the NHL. He ranked in stature with Gretzky and Lemieux. He became regarded as the second greatest offensive player in the franchise's history, after only Gordie Howe. In 1988-89, Yzerman scored 65 goals. In other seasons, he scored 62, 58, 51 and 50 goals. Howe had 49 in his best goal-scoring season.

The sport, of course, was different when Howe played it. Schedules were shorter. There were six teams, all skilled. Expansion created a 26-team league, diluted in talent.

But Howe had won the Stanley Cup four times.

When Bowman became the Red Wings' coach in 1993, one of his earliest machinations was to try to recreate Yzerman. Bowman wanted a fast, slick defensive forward, one adept at forechecking. Yzerman never complained. But he did not thrill to the change.

He still scored, but never with the production of the earlier years. So the critics harped. The trade rumors proliferated.

There had been reports that he would be traded after the Red Wings lost in the playoffs in 1994 to San Jose. They vanished without merit.

But such rumors were wildly pounced upon after the Jersey sweep for the Cup in 1995. The Ottawa Senators made an overture for Yzerman. He was a hometown player. They had a general manager, Randy Sexton, who was on the cusp, trying to salvage his job. The Senators had a new rink and needed a name player to lure fans inside. Rumors were floated in Ottawa, printed as a done deal. They were refloated in Detroit.

Yzerman fretted. The Senators were an expansion team with a dubious future. They were mismanaged.

The trade rumors proliferated. Out of character, at a practice session before the season opened in 1995, Yzerman lost his temper. He threw his stick. He barked at the media.

As it turned out, he wasn't traded. The rumors had slammed out of control, based on Ottawa's wishful thinking. Two high-echelon sources on the Red Wings confirmed that an Yzerman trade was never seriously close. Jimmy Devellano, a Detroit club vice-president, said the Red Wings had stacked the price so high for Yzerman that the Senators could never afford to make such a deal.

Two things happened in the aftermath.

Yzerman mused about the media, still miffed.

"Don't they have any accountability?" he said one day.

The second thing that happened was that Mike Ilitch, the club owner, signed him to a contract that bound him to the Red Wings for the duration of his career. It would pay $17.5 million over four seasons, and guaranteed a front-office job when Yzerman retired as a player.

That night, Yzerman celebrated. He had a goal and three assists.

Perhaps, of all the goals he has scored — 539 in the regular season and and 46 in the playoffs — his finest, his most sensational was in the 1996 playoffs. A seven-game struggle with the St. Louis Blues went into double overtime. Yzerman ended it with a blazing shot. He spun around behind the net with all his teammates on top of him, thumping his back.

That would be surpassed by the goal he scored against the Avalanche in the second game of the 1997 Western Conference finals. The Red Wings had lost the first game and had trailed, 2-0, in the second. Quickly, they were in position for another disappointment. Detroit tied it. Yzerman set up Fedorov for the tying goal.

With four minutes left, Yzerman got the puck in the Detroit zone, sped through center, around the Colorado defense. From behind the net he shoved the puck at goalie Patrick Roy. It went in off Roy's leg. It would become the most vital goal of Yzerman's 14 seasons in Detroit.

It turned around the series. From then on, the Red Wings were dominant against Colorado — losing only one more game — and over Philadelphia — losing none. Yzerman had another key goal in the first game of the Finals, the long-distance shot that doomed the Flyers.

Several years ago, the Canadiens signed Patrick Roy to a contract paying $4 million a season. To justify such a sum at that time, Serge Savard, then Canadiens' general manager, explained to Montreal reporters that Roy had won Stanley Cups, "a guy like Yzerman has never won anything."

But now it has happened. The Captain has his Cup.

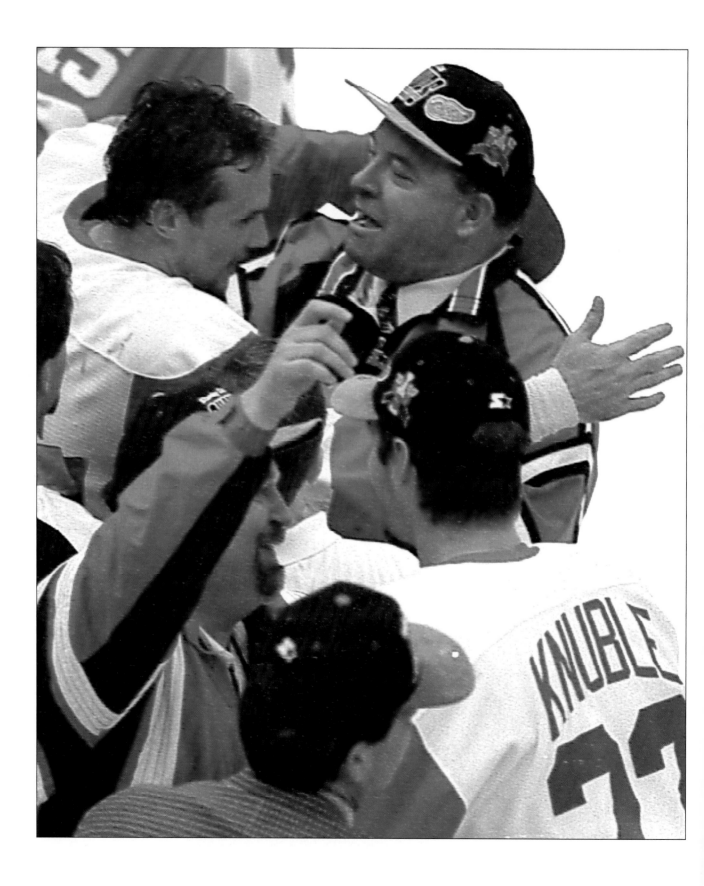

The Coach

At 63, Bowman changed himself, and changed Wings into winners

BY JERRY GREEN

The Detroit News

I t is a dangerous game. The players carry clubs in their hands. They wear honed steel blades as sharp as knives on their feet. They dash crazily on ice and shoot a galvanized rubber disc wildly at speeds above 100 miles an hour. In an earlier era, they did not wear protective helmets.

It is the game Scotty Bowman aspired to play in the National Hockey League, since he was a wee lad in an English-speaking neighborhood of Montreal. He possessed the talent for the game. It was evident he was NHL material by the time he reached junior hockey in his late teens.

Then — Bowman relishes retelling his life story — the accident that turned him into coaching. He sat one day during hockey season in the back room where the Red Wings coaches view videos and diagram defenses. The room is reporter-proof. A rare invitation was issued. And he spoke:

"I got my first skates when I was maybe seven. That was pretty young in those days. You didn't get on teams until you were around 12. I got on a team when I was around 10. I played when I was seven, but we didn't have organized teams.

"I got on a group team when I was about 14. We won the whole province of Quebec midget championship."

He advanced to the Montreal Royals, the Canadiens' top junior club. One day, on the ice, there was a collision. Two players carrying those clubs, riding on those steel knife-sharp blades. Bowman received a severe whack in the head. His skull was shattered. His career ambitions were crushed.

He loved hockey so he steered into coaching, where he would become an immortal. He would coach the great Canadiens to five Stanley Cup champions in his native Montreal. He would coach the Pittsburgh Penguins to another Stanley Cup championship in 1992. And at age 63, after bitter disappointments, he would recreate, mastermind, tinker with the Red

Scotty Bowman embraces his team captain, Steve Yzerman, after winning the Stanley Cup.

Wings until they were molded into his ideal of a championship team. And they would win the Stanley Cup in 1997 for the first time in 42 years.

Coach of seven Stanley Cup champions, player development director of another, the ironic result of a knock in the head. Only Toe Blake, of the mighty Canadiens in the 1950's and 60's, coached more Stanley Cup champions than Bowman, eight.

"A player was all I wanted to be," he said, continuing his story in the back room in the bowels of Joe Louis Arena. "I went to high school but ... Actually when I got injured, I was still in high school. It was my senior year. I was playing junior hockey. I got injured March 7, 1951. I was 18 ½."

There was a skirmish. Scotty was hit over the head by a stick. He fell to the ice, badly hurt. The player who whacked Bowman over the head with the hockey stick was a young defenseman, Jean-Guy Talbot. Bowman would never forget the name.

Young coaches are required to begin at the bottom, the roots of hockey across Canada. Bowman started with kids' hockey, junior B's, juniors in Ottawa, the Peterborough Petes, the junior Canadiens. In 1967, the NHL expanded, doubled in size from The Original Six. There were six head coaching positions instantly available.

Bowman was hired by Lynn Patrick to coach the new St. Louis Blues.

His players were craggy veterans, their careers prolonged by new job opportunities. Bowman had two brilliant hockey Hall of Famers to play goal, Glenn Hall and Jacques Plante. He had Dickie Moore and Doug Harvey, two aging players from the Canadiens past champions.

But in this first season, Bowman sought another veteran defenseman.

Bowman's NHL record

Year	Team	Regular Season			Playoffs	
		W	L	T	W	L
1967-68	St. Louis	23	21	14	8	10
1968-69	St. Louis	37	25	14	8	4
1969-70	St. Louis	32	7	12	8	8
1970-71	St. Louis	13	10	5	2	4
1971-72	Montreal	46	16	16	2	4
1972-73	Montreal*	52	10	16	12	5
1973-74	Montreal	45	24	9	2	4
1974-75	Montreal	47	14	19	6	5
1975-76	Montreal*	58	11	11	12	1
1976-77	Montreal*	60	8	12	12	2
1977-78	Montreal*	59	10	11	12	3
1978-79	Montreal*	52	17	11	12	4
1979-80	Buffalo	47	17	16	9	5
1981-82	Buffalo	18	10	7	1	3
1982-83	Buffalo	38	28	14	2	3
1983-84	Buffalo	48	25	7	0	3
1984-85	Buffalo	38	28	14	2	3
1985-86	Buffalo	18	18	1	0	0
1986-87	Buffalo	3	7	2	0	0
1991-92	Pittsburgh*	39	32	9	16	5
1992-93	Pittsburgh	56	21	7	7	5
1993-94	Detroit	46	30	8	3	4
1994-95	Detroit	33	11	4	12	6
1995-96	Detroit	62	13	7	10	9
1996-97	Detroit*	36	26	18	16	4
TOTAL		1.011	460	263	178	105

* Stanley Cup champions

He scanned the NHL's waiver wire. He picked a name.

The player he brought to the blues was an ornery craggy, tough, veteran defenseman. His name was Jean-Guy Talbot.

The irony was rich. They never discussed the incident that had terminated Bowman's career as a player at its beginning 16 years earlier.

He developed the elderly Blues into a team that reached the Stanley Cup Finals the first three years of their existence. The NHL, in its desire

Avalanche Coach
Marc Crawford had
plenty to say, but
Bowman had the
last laugh in the
Western Conference
finals. The Wings
beat Colorado in six
games to advance to
the Stanley Cup
Finals.

to market the United States, rigged the playoffs so that an American expansion club would reach the Finals every year. Scotty's Blues never won a game against the established Canadiens or Bruins in three championship series.

But he was established as an NHL coach. His jut-jawed image, head held upward, reaching down for an ice cube to munch, would become a television caricature for more than a quarter century.

Bowman was coveted by Charles O. Finley to coach the California Seals and Jack Kent Cooke to coach the Los Angeles Kings. He rejected both owners. He would ultimately return to Montreal. He had proven, in signing Talbot, that he did not necessarily have to love his players to win. Many of them have proven through the years that they certainly didn't love him.

In Detroit, there was a huge generation gap. Bowman had the credentials, he had the hockey knowledge, but it was uncertain that he had the knack to handle athletes 35 and 40 years younger than he was. He has been successful through the 1960's, an era of young rage, and the 1970's, 80's into the 90's. The character of North American youth changed. Salaries climbed and climbed. Athletes needed pampering. The dressing room often turned into a sandbox.

Plus there was another gap. This gap was transoceanic. The Red Wings were avidly signing

Bowman always wanted to be an NHL star, but after he suffered a head injury during a game, he was forced into switching to another career — coaching.

Europeans. They brought in players from Sweden. When the Soviet Union crumbled in 1989, skillful Russian hockey players suddenly found they were free to become millionaires. The Red Wings quickly signed players from Moscow's famed CSKA champions, the noted Red Army team. They picked off Sergei Fedorov, Vladimir Konstantinov, Vyacheslav Kozlov. All for free. Valerie Gushin, the general manager of the Red Army team in Moscow, cried American piracy. The Red Wings laughed in response.

Bowman handled athletes of mixed personalities, sulkers and carousers, for 25 years in the NHL. But Russians — and the Red Wings would have a Russian Five when they won the Stanley Cup — would be a different sort of challenge.

Sitting in the room, Bowman pointed to one of the five Russians.

"He had a lifestyle orgasm," Bowman said. "He had no idea five years ago he'd have what he has now."

When Bowman arrived in Detroit in 1993, he had just won his sixth Cup as a coach in Pittsburgh. He became the Detroit coach with the simple mandate from franchise owner Mike Ilitich:

"Win the Cup."

It took four seasons of grooming, retooling, cajoling, surviving front office politics — and changing some playing lifestyles. It took four years of carping, and rumors, from much of the media. It took four years of playing goalkeeper tag.

"My idol in hockey was Toe Blake," said Bowman. "But the coach I admired was Don Shula. He lasted a long time. He had to change styles."

But more often, Bowman had been compared to another historic, despot-ic football coach in moods, temperament, handling of athletes.

"He is the best coach in any sport since Vince Lombardi," a journalist familiar with both eras said during the 1996-97 season.

It was the ultimate compliment.

Bowman's first three seasons with the Red Wings were shocking, disappointing, frustrating, controversial, at times angry.

Ilitch hired Bowman after Jacques Demers and then Bryan Murray were given the ziggy — a Detroit-only word that translates to an unceremonious firing. Demers and Murray had moderate success. Murray spent three years as coach and general manager. After failures in the playoffs, he was replaced by Bowman, but retained the GM's position.

The Red Wings had stars. Bowman inherited Steve Yzerman, the club's captain. At the time, Yzerman was regarded in the same scoring echelon as Mario Lemieux and Wayne Gretzky. Yzerman had seasons in which he had scored 50, 65, 62, 51 and 58 goals.

One of Bowman's first acts was to change Yzerman's style. A swift, elusive skater, Bowman had Yzerman concentrate on defense.

The Red Wings finished first in the Western Conference in Bowman's first season. They were humiliated in the first round of the playoffs by the lightweight San Jose Sharks.

Ilitch impatiently courted Mike Keenan, who had just won the Cup with the Rangers, to switch to Detroit as coach. The Blues outbid the Red Wings for Keenan. Bowman survived.

What the Red Wings had was two coach/GM types, Bowman and Murray. One naturally had to go. Murray was fired. Bowman assumed his basic duties as director of player personnel.

His second season, the Red Wings reached the Cup Finals for the first time in 29 years. Detroit was agog with hockey enthusiasm. The Red Wings were favored to win the Stanley Cup against the New Jersey Devils, once referred to as "a Mickey Mouse team" by Wayne Gretzky. Detroit hadn't won it since 1955. The Devils blew the Red Wings out in a horrendous four-game sweep.

Shawn Burr was made the scapegoat. He was traded to Tampa Bay.

Burr told The St. Petersburg Times what happened once when Bowman called him for an opinion of the coaching.

"Scotty, you're 60 years old," Burr was quoted as saying. "You play with toy trains. You use a duck call to make line changes. People call you a genius. I think there's something wrong with you. I think you're a joke."

In Bowman's third season the Red Wings roared through the schedule. They had a target — the magic sports number of 60. In all of NHL history only one club had won 60 games in a season. It was the 1976-77 Canadiens, coached by Scotty Bowman. It was the second of Bowman's four-season Cup dynasty in Montreal. The Red Wings broke the record with 62 victories.

He can be a secretive man with a deep curiosity.

This time the Red Wings were eliminated in a heated, nasty six-game semifinal, or Western Conference final, series with the Colorado Avalanche. Bowman enraged, engaged in a nasty parking lot shouting match in Denver with the Avalanche's Claude Lemieux.

"Nice sucker punch, Lemieux,"

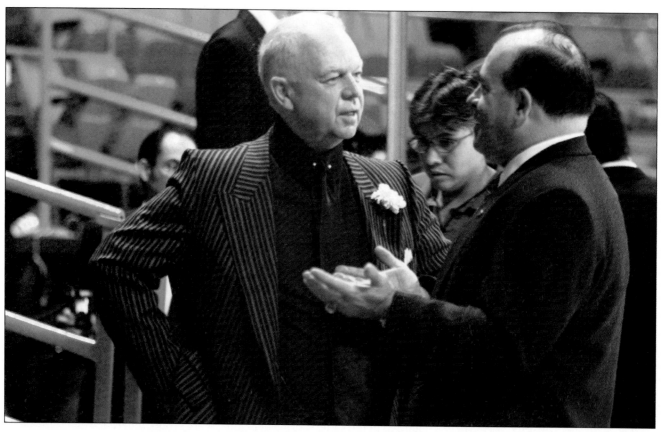

Don Cherry, left, and Bowman had one thing in common: They each coached a Cup champion.

Bowman was heard to yell from the Red Wings' bus.

For the first time, Marc Crawford, the young Colorado coach, spouted angry remarks at Bowman.

"He's the master of creating a little bit of circus away from the game ..." Crawford told the media.

"He's been doing this thing for years and years and years ...

"He's a great thinker, but he thinks so much that you even get the plate in his head causing interference on our headsets during the game."

It was a cruel remark. One of the myths in the NHL is that Bowman has a plate in his head because of the incident with Talbot.

Some of Bowman's old Montreal players who went on to high posts in

hockey spoke with praise. Former All-Star defenseman Larry Robinson is now coach of the Kings.

"Hate is the wrong word, but when he was coaching us, he wasn't a guy you as a player respected," Robinson told the Los Angeles Times. "But you respect him now more that you're through. To you, it's a game. To him, it's much more than that. He's always trying to stay a step ahead. He's constantly thinking of ways to make you a better player. I guess I misunderstood when I was a player. But being in his shoes now, I understand a lot better why he did the things he did."

It was the highest tribute a former player could give to his former coach.

Ken Dryden, Bowman's Montreal goalkeeper, now is boss of the Maple Leafs.

"The only common piece is Scotty Bowman, and that says a lot," Dryden said while the Red Wings were aiming to break the 60-victories record.

Beaten again in the playoffs by Colorado, Bowman again reformed his club for 1996-97. This time the club was created to win the playoffs. The regular season was simply regarded as a testing period. They finished second in the division, third in the conference.

Bowman had a grander scheme. He dealt popular Dino Ciccarelli to Tampa Bay. "He's a jerk," Ciccarelli said publicly. He cashiered Bob Errey.

"A man that doesn't respect people should not be given any respect," Errey told The St.Petersburg Times. "Why would you want time for a man like that."

Bowman shrugged off the criticism.

He dealt Paul Coffey and Keith Primeau to Hartford to obtain a huge property the Red Wings desperately needed — Brendan Shanahan. He brought Joey Kocur back from a suburban Detroit beer league to provide muscle. He played the five Russians as a unit — Fedorov, Kozlov, Igor Larionov, Konstantinov, Slava Fetisov. Then he broke them up. Unlike the year before, when he played guessing games whether Chris Osgood or Mike Vernon would start playoff games, he settled on a single goalkeeper. He relegated the younger Osgood to the bench and went with the experienced Vernon. To shore up the defense, he obtained Larry Murphy from the Maple Leafs.

And when playoffs came, the Red Wings were prepared. They rolled through. They beat St. Louis in six. They swept Anaheim, with three games going into overtime. After a triple overtime victory, Bowman even showed some emotion. He smiled. They evened matters with Colorado, Bowman admonishing Crawford during one evening of belligerence in Joe Louis Arena.

William Scott Bowman, himself, had revered his father. He was the son of a Scottish immigrant in a bilingual city. It is rather difficult to picture Scotty Bowman, as a little boy, playing with the kids down the street, wearing his Boston Bruins' replica jersey, in the 1930's and early 1940's.

Young Scotty Bowman, perverse even as a lad, favored neither the Canadiens nor the Maroons, soon to be disbanded.

"I grew up a Boston Bruin fan," Bowman said in his back room, "the reason being the Boston radio broadcast. You could pick up the signal in Montreal. I think the reason was, I was about seven years old, and they were winning the Cup. The Rangers won it in '40. Boston won it in '41.

"I used to have to go to bed at the end of the first or second period. My father would always write the score before he went to work the next day.

"I think probably the reason that I was a Boston fan, they were a strong team. One Christmas I got ... somehow they found a Boston Bruins jersey.

"The two jerseys you could buy in Montreal were Canadiens and Toronto. They found a Boston Bruins jersey and they put No. 10 on it for Bill Cowley. That was my big hero. He was a big centerman, as you know. He made more wings than Boeing. From Ottawa. Died a couple of years ago. I visited him.

"There was nobody else around me who followed the Bruins. You're kids, you can't get into much trouble. I used to wear my Boston sweater."

This was Scotty Bowman in his off-ice finest, the raconteur, the historian.

Bowman's street in suburban Verdun was part French-speaking and part-English speaking. He learned both languages, attended a French-speaking school for while. All the kids rooted for the Canadiens and Maroons, except Bowman — and the two kids down the street with their other interests.

"The first game I would have gone to was Canadiens against Maroons,"

Bowman said, "Because my father was a Maroons fan.

"See, when you grew up in Montreal at that time, most of the English were Maroons fans. The French were for the Canadiens ...

"They had what they called in Montreal at the time, they had a rush end. Fifty cents. They called it Millionaires' Row, but it (cost only) 50 cents.

"I remember my dad waited, he used to line up behind the Forum. Obviously in the middle of winter, and he waited for tickets ... Tickets were sold at the corner of Burnside and Atwater. Right on the corner, they had a little wicket there.

Jack Bowman was a soccer player and a blacksmith by trade in Scotland. He emigrated to Canada in 1929. He became a railroad man. In 1930, Bowman's mother, Jean, went to Montreal to marry Jack.

It was from his mother, Jean, that Bowman inherited much of his personality. There were times, it has been reported, that she would respond to weak hands in card games by throwing her cards into the fireplace.

"I grew up on a street, two of the boys became safecrackers," he said once. "They would crack safes. In banks.

"That wasn't the real type of neighborhood it was."

Scotty Bowman did not achieve his boyhood ambition. But his playmates from down the street in Verdun did.

"One ended up in prison in Vancouver," Bowman said, "and the other ended up in the big job (big house) in Boston. They became bank robbers. Armed robbery."

And Bowman collected eight precious Stanley Cup rings.

MEET THE RED WINGS

An inside look at the 1997 Stanley Cup champions

DOUG BROWN

Right wing
Height: 5-10
Weight: 185
Born: June 12, 1964.

MATHIEU DANDENAULT

Right wing
Height: 5-10
Weight: 185
Born: June 12, 1964.

KRIS DRAPER

Center
Height: 5-11
Weight: 185
Born: May 24, 1971.

SERGEI FEDOROV

Center
Height: 6-1
Weight: 200
Born: December 13, 1969.

SLAVA FETISOV

Defenseman
Height: 6-1
Weight: 215
Born: April 20, 1958

KEVIN HODSON

Goalie
Height: 6-0
Weight: 178
Born: March 27, 1972

TOMAS HOLMSTROM

Left Wing
Height: 6-0
Weight: 200
Born: January 23, 1973

MIKE KNUBLE

Right Wing
Height: 6-3
Weight: 216
Born: July 4, 1972

JOE KOCUR

Right Wing
Height: 6-0
Weight: 205
Born: December 21, 1964

VLADIMIR KONSTANTINOV

Defenseman
Height: 6-0
Weight: 195
Born: March 19, 1967

VYACHESLAV KOZLOV

Left Wing
Height: 5-10
Weight: 185
Born: May 3, 1972

MARTIN LAPOINTE

Right Wing
Height: 5-11
Weight: 200
Born: September 12, 1973